YOU
Are
Worth Saving

Letters of Hope from a Desperate Heart

♡ *Stacee*

STACEE GOETZINGER

ISBN 978-1-64114-275-5 (Paperback)
ISBN 978-1-64114-276-2 (Digital)

Christian Faith Publishing, Inc.
296 Chestnut Street
Meadville, PA 16335
www.christianfaithpublishing.com

Scriptures taken from the Holy Bible, New International Version, NIV. © 1973, 1978, 1984, 2011 by Biblica, Inc. Used by permission of Zondervan. All rights reserved worldwide. www.zondervan.com The NIV and New International Version are trademarks registered in the United States Patent and Trademark Office by Biblica, Inc.

Cover image was taken by Makenzie Magnus
photographedbymakenzie@gmail.com

Printed in the United States of America

To my precious sister Tracee,

    May we never let the giggles of sneaking turkey sandwiches on late summer nights ever become anything but a good memory. You've never left me behind, Trace.

    I love you forever.

Contents

Introduction

I am imbalanced! Or at least that's what they say. I don't produce serotonin without the assistance of medication, and when I don't take my medicine, I go to a very dark place. This doesn't change until I re-medicate. I, with doctor's assistance, have tried numerous times to go off of my daily regimen of medication, but it doesn't work. I have chosen to use depression as my friend because it draws me closer to God. I'll explain later. I have anorexia nervosa and need God for every bite. I have had issues with self-harm and most specifically cutting. I have guilt. Because of how I was created and as a result of having these challenges, I can get lost mentally in what I am intended to hear. There is, I suppose, a glitch in the process. The words and my response sometimes just don't match up and I need help with what's going on or I become "lost in the translations that I need to understand." My ever so qualified helpers through this process? God, my patient husband, doctors, close family members, and my closest of friends. They are better known as "my translators." Tireless encouragers in their help as my conversation partners.

Twenty-four hours was the magic number I was posed with. Was I going to stay with my mom and move to Dallas, Texas, or stay with my dad in Apple Valley, California? I was a senior in high school who had moved two times already and I felt apathetic. Extroverted, childlike, chatty, became silenced, overwhelmed, sad. I have loved both of my parents relentlessly, but I knew my mom needed me and I went. I went to Texas and was the new girl once again. I went from average student trying to keep up when getting to a new school, to struggling to care if I even graduated. Competitive tennis player, to after-school career girl at odd jobs and missing my dad and sister and worried sick about my mom even though our rooms in the tiny apartment shared a wall.

I did…I felt older than seventeen. My family of four had made it through thirteen moves, two dogs, numerous churches, leaving friends, making new ones, laughs, tears, anger, hunkering down together, and then occasionally there were explosions. My parents' marriage ended and had taken its toll on all of us in very different ways. I'm the pleaser and peacemaker, the optimist… and was tired of life as it had been the last few years especially, although still in the prime of my teenage years. I concluded that I was not successful in using my role in my family and I was upset at the possibilities of what life was about to look like. Like your family, sometimes we were a complete puzzle together, the four of us, with God as the centerpiece, but often there were missing pieces so the picture just wasn't clear and we all went our separate ways emotionally.

We were all split up and I wanted my family back but it was too late.

I'm very sensitive. Always have been. I've been a Christian since I was just a little girl and I came from a Christian home, but being a Christian doesn't mean that all is well, and you know this. It means that we have free choice and it is wise to choose Jesus because whether things in your life and my life stay together, or burst into a million tiny pieces, we need help. I've always been very perceptive and I have longed to help others whether I knew them or not. I'm not fearful, so I have to rely on God and the instincts he has given to me to stay out of trouble. I have a lead foot when I drive and God has to slow me down in the car and in life. I've felt like a grown-up most of my life so I can feel like a kid or a teen these days but since I'm the mom of teens, it's important for me to be careful!

I Am a Perfect Storm…maybe to those who have read this introduction thus far. I know! Looks bleak! Doesn't it? In the conversation of life, I am a walking and breathing mess without God in the math problem called my life. This is one equation I actually know the answer to, however! The answer in my life is Jesus. He is why I write. He is the introduction and the conclusion to this book of my sharing in a raw yet hopeful way of me making it through each meal, and each emotion, each day.

I hope the description of me makes you feel better about you! Don't worry, it gets better! But whether it does or not, I want you to know something: we were meant to go through things at times with God alone, but often we are meant to go through things in life with others. We were created to live in community and draw one another back to the only one who can fix us. My life, you will see, is full of God's grace, and you are not alone when you let others in. I've found that people that God puts in our lives are a lot less shocked about my issues, and that their responses are a lot less often nothing like I expected because they have issues too!

Let's try something opposite of what we are accustomed to perhaps. Let's put our guard down just a touch and look at hope in the midst of whatever is going on in our lives. We all have struggles and secrets that can make us sick when the door is shut on them, and locked, and the key is somewhere on a counter under papers that we have no desire to go through. Buried hurts are like a paralysis that we get used to and spend a great deal of time compensating for! What if together, one moment at a time, we give God our hurts and struggles and begin to learn a new way to live.

Following this page, are thirty letters that may find you tired beyond your years and apathetic at least. Here, I have shared about the reality of and hope in my days and how I don't even get up until I've confessed that I cannot make even a successful decision without Jesus. The alternative is more times than not, a fail. I've tried to do life alone and it doesn't work for me. God has brought restoration to my family and joy in the good and not-so-good days. Please join me and read the following pages whether it be all the way through or one per day. I pray with all that I am that you are encouraged by how God shows me hope in the midst of a yelling mind. "I will not die but live and will proclaim what the lord has done." (Ps. 118:17).

Let's commit to life one day at a time...together, whether we share the same hurts and challenges, or not. Wow! It's a privilege to have you join me in the journey God has me on and what an honor to be invited to be a part of yours! Let's get better together!

Speak Out Loud

Dear Friend,

Some time ago, a friend showed me this verse: "I will not die but live, and will proclaim what the Lord has done" (Ps. 118:17). I have loved these words for several years now, but only recently have they been a source of courage to speak out loud about God's relentless grace and mercy in my life. For years I have let an eating disorder speak for me, so you can only imagine how communicating in writing sort of feels like I am yelling!

I already know it is worth it because of the hope I have: that you too can fight to live the life God has for you. Not too long ago, I reached a point of absolute exhaustion, as if I was climbing a wall that was only getting higher. I just couldn't do it anymore. I sat down on the floor of my bedroom and just cried out to Jesus. I physically opened my hands, asking Him to take it all—all my pride in the eating disorder, all the fear of not punishing myself anymore for being a poor example…just everything. I am so glad I was sitting on the floor, because I was so humbled by our communication and the peace He gave me. Jesus never ever responds to us as we deserve.

I choose to speak out loud—to address my fight against the mental torture I have let the enemy inflict on me for more years than I can recall. God has given me the desire not only to live, but to thrive—and the tactics needed to do so. As I speak out loud, I recognize the power our words carry. They are not the words I am used to, but I am adjusting! The desire to truly live is relatively new for me, but God's words to me are life-giving. I've been "merely existing" exceptionally well, and these days of reading may begin with the temptation for you to merely exist, but I pray that you will not close this book feeling that way. These pages are about possibly thriving for the first time in my life, and in yours.

I am not writing these words as someone who is a counselor or authority on depression and medication, eating disorders or self-abuse. I am a wife and mom, a daughter and friend, a sister and a child of God who has lived with these issues, and who gets up every single day refusing to let any of these weaknesses make me want to die more than live. But with surrender, changes do come; and God is carrying me to a life of absolute amazement in Him and in my value in His eyes.

I sometimes see you when I am at the grocery store, recitals, malls, and church, and I can hear you silently saying, "I don't want to disappear, but I am struggling with all that I am just to live." Yes, I see you, and I've been there with that same silent scream; but most importantly, God sees you just as He sees me. He sees you and has a plan for you greater than you can fathom. I have not arrived in my healing or in daily overcoming and, honestly, some days are better than others. But when I allow my days to have a change of course, it is because I have chosen to be rescued by Jesus Himself, not by a Diet Coke (my caffeine fix)—and I do so much better! As I am relearning to live, I hope the rawness that comes through resonates with you and gives you the courage to speak out loud—to others who need to hear *you* speak hope into their lives.

Love to you,
Stacee

Never Too Much

Dear Friend,

Are you struggling today? I am, too, and I have let more days than I can count slip into the hands of the enemy. Today, if we will stop our current rituals, the day can be handed to Jesus. But you and I have some choices to make at this moment, so that we do not fall into addictive behavior or let the enemy have control of our thoughts and choices. God our Father understands where we are emotionally today, and He wants us to let ourselves do what does *not* come naturally. It is essential to let Him into our hurt and distress. He longs to go to our pain, our habitual thoughts of negativity. Stop agreeing with the enemy! It's easier to believe his lies when we are down, but he is no less toxic then.

Let me tell you (and remind myself) of a new concept in my life: we were *not* created for abuse. So where is Jesus right now as we hurt? He is waiting with anticipation to go to our souls and, with His strong but gentle hand, touch each wound. No wound is too deep, sweet friend. When I was a little girl I had long red hair, and when I was sad or felt like I was too much to handle, I would sit on the floor beside my bed and wish for someone I loved and trusted to stroke my hair and relieve my mind…to tell me I *wasn't* too much to handle… that what I thought about myself wasn't true…that my needs could be met without a fight.

Now, as a grown-up, I can still feel the same way. My heart can hurt and feel inconsolable, and I can be sure I am too much for even God to handle. I can hear this is a lie, but when I invite Him into my hurt and struggle, healing and hope come over me deeper than any human's soothing touch. Word pictures are used throughout the Bible because God knew we would need them. He wants us to learn through identification. It's really a brilliant part of our makeup. Use this ability to picture letting Jesus come to you. He is here, He is now, and He is never overwhelmed by my life. Let Jesus see you and me vulnerable in this moment. Let Him in to console you and give you hope by touching your wounds one by one. He is not afraid. He is able.

Please, just one day at a time, choose Jesus's perspective on you and your life. We have to try—I have found that if I am able to memorize the hate words the enemy yells at me, I can memorize the opposite. Change can be scary and very frustrating, so let me show you some perspective-changing words: "For I am the LORD your God who takes hold of your right hand and says to you, Do not fear; I will help you" (Isa. 41:13). For all of the things I have done to hurt myself, maybe today I could purposefully choose to let Him help me.

Love to you,
Stacee

Deeper Waters

Dear Friend,

I confess that I cannot do life on my own. I've tried, and it doesn't work out for me. After doing my morning errands, I purposefully went to our local lake to stop and get alone with Jesus. We are in the middle of a drought, so our lake is more of a pond-ish puddle, but it is still breathtaking, especially when there is at least one sailboat working its way to deeper waters. I found myself drawn to a bench on the other side of a lighthouse where there were some large rocks, and I just sat down. The breeze was perfect—it made my hair fall across my eyes, then my face. I closed my eyes and just thought about the Lord. Sitting out there, I wasn't hurting. My mind wasn't thinking abusive thoughts. The sun was shining on my freckled face, and it felt life-giving and good to me.

In my time with Jesus, I've been reading about being so close with Him that we are sitting side by side. That's when He imparts His heart, His wisdom about my life. That's what I want. I desire to be so close with Him that He can whisper and my ear will catch His next step for my life. For more than twenty-five years I have heard an eating disorder scream at me, telling me not to eat a bite…that I don't deserve to eat. That's my normal, so this is the opposite in my life. I *want* opposite. I will work for it and wait for it, because this means I can have a chance at really living life today. I'm going in a new direction. I am seeking revelation for deep healing. Surface healing is painful and temporary.

As I sat there longer, I briefly opened my eyes; they were drawn to a tall bird to my left, and I began to laugh. There was a crane standing in shallow mud…just stuck. I so know how you feel, Miss Crane! There is so much water on this earth, but you are stuck in the mud in a drought where there used to be deep water! Please, Jesus… I've been stuck in the pit of wrong choices, and it hurts. The enemy wants me to believe there is no deep relationship to be had with You—that there are no longer deep waters available for a person like me. But I see differently. I see hope in the lives of others who have obeyed You and listened to You so much that they overflow from being side by side with You, Lord. Needless to say, today I am determined *not* to be the crane!

"Show me Your ways, O Lord, teach me Your paths; guide me in Your truth and teach me, for You are God my Savior, and my hope is in You all day long" (Ps. 25:4-5).

As I am writing this letter, God is bringing about some changes in my life. There are days when I still feel stuck in the mud, but I'm learning to experience more and more of the hope found in God's deeper waters. Please know and accept that Jesus has this for you!

Love to you,
Stacee

Beyond Survival

Dear Friend,

Not too long ago, I sat in a small, glass-walled room. The view through the window—gorgeous green and orange leaves in a forest of trees—went on as far as I could see. Though wanting to stay focused on the foliage, I was fighting deep emotions, and I became distracted by the conversations occurring in pockets around me. I was exhausted but interested in what was being said. I moved to a sofa by the window, alone...but still close enough to be included. As one conversation faded, I became engaged in another.

The first girl I met was nineteen, a college student, and newly away from home, facing a lot of new pressures. Right after the semester began, her boyfriend of two years abruptly broke up with her. Overwhelmed by this broken relationship, she became depressed and turned to bulimia. She was lonely in her new situation, and the bulimia was a distraction. She was afraid of not fitting in. What if she couldn't?

A young girl with long blond hair sat alone. She was responsive toward others' comments but that was all. She made no verbal connection unless directly spoken to and, even then, her answers were short, tired. She lived at home with her mom and sister, and right after high school she had begun working full time at a nursing home. Her days were long. She just couldn't leave an elderly friend in a wet or dirty bed, so she stayed until she felt her job was done. She was a sweet girl who had trouble saying "no" and the integrity to complete her daily tasks at minimal pay. She became exhausted and overworked.

A little redheaded Greek lady, very well-spoken and sophisticated, made her way over to sit next to me. She was spunky and funny. Her voice carried throughout the little glass room, but she was confident and didn't mind. She was a high school principal, a proud grandma. Her joy? She claimed it came from Jesus. Nevertheless, unspoken life disappointment had taken a toll on her, and pills for depression had become too many... too frequent.

A young man, humble and unassuming, around twenty-two, walked up. He was supposed to be graduating from college and on his way to medical school, but his family's expectations to follow previous generations of doctors were too much. He was disappointed in himself for failing at this tradition, and he believed others were, too—others he cared about so deeply. Depression and overwhelming fears of failure put him into a dark hole mentally.

The person I came to know last, but perhaps best, was intimidating to me. She was guarded, missing her husband and little girls who she barely got to kiss goodbye—many days ago, it seemed. Although outwardly engaged in the group, she was hurting deeply and her mind was relentless with shameful thoughts. Her body was weak; her hollow face was striving to show the desire to live, but not as life was currently. Hard knocks long before her marriage had been tolerable until now. Outgoing melted into not going, and agreement with negative thoughts from the enemy when she made a mistake was a given. Praying Scriptures and recalling God's promises were prominent in her life, yet the fog of oppression would not lift. In this new environment she felt safe, understood, helped.

The way our bodies function, the way our minds work, is very delicate. Depression, anxiety, and chemical imbalances are real. My mind actually stopped producing enough serotonin, and I got sick. The last person I describe above...was me. I became exhausted from being a grown-up well before my time. I kept trying to run ahead of the things I needed to let God heal, but I couldn't run anymore; and I became sick enough to be placed in the intensive care unit of a mental hospital. I didn't eat by myself, go to the restroom by myself, or rest alone during my stay. My pretty shoes were now held closed by black tape so that I wouldn't use the laces to hurt myself. Each time I looked down, I saw the tape and felt scared of myself; but I was alive, and this was where I needed to be. I wanted so much to just hold my redheaded girls and be a godly mom. I desperately wanted to be the minister's wife who had it all together—or at least something together, like those I served with. But I wasn't. I felt old and used up and discouraged that I had to be good for enough days to earn my razor back, so I could shave the legs that had finally stopped running.

Although this hospital did have extreme cases, I was mostly surrounded by people like you and me. They were precious, and they were fighters—or perhaps they wouldn't have made it to the hospital. All of my life I have been a pleaser and a peacemaker. I have cared deeply, and I have loved deeply. I have struggled deeply, and I have served God deeply; but I have also been suicidal because my mind hurt, and I thought I was failing those around me—in my view, deeply.

But little by little, I'm seeing this wasn't God's view; and since He has loved me before I was even "Stacee," He knows just how to heal me deeply. This melts me! Here's the truth: I am not an isolated case. These days of isolation were part of me coming to the point where I could begin to say, "I'm afraid and I need Your help, Jesus!" In my weakness and brokenness, He ushered in His strength and compassion, and I can see that now. He will do the same for you! Right where you are, you are not alone. Please know that Jesus sees you, and He loves you, and He has a plan for you that far surpasses survival.

Please read these words today: "For you created my inmost being; you knit me together in my mother's womb. I praise you because I am fearfully and wonderfully made; your works are wonderful, I know that full well" (Ps. 139:13-14).

Love to you,
Stacee

Doing Life

Dear Friend,

This morning I got up and quickly decided to lie back down. Could I do life today? I wrapped myself tightly in the soft covers that always welcome me and closed my eyes hard. I knew what my mind would chant, and I knew I would have the choice to combat it with Scriptures, whether or not I committed to a day standing upright. Change takes so much energy—especially when one of the changes is to obey God and eat. The thing I habitually resist is the very thing that keeps me alive: food. I don't want to lose another moment of another day; and when I wake up and my head hurts pretty badly, it reminds me that I am not eating enough, so I am dehydrated. Not a great reality to start my day, but this can change—because when I commit to honor God and eat, I am not a slave to the eating disorder.

One eye at a time reopened tentatively. On the wall adjacent to my bed is a huge lime green (yep, lime green!) poster I made a few years ago. I posted this large reminder on my wall for reasons having nothing to do with decorating! In my fight to become what I believe—new thoughts and truths rather than the absolute lies—I have to practice! I have these reminders up all around our house. My family has adjusted to my "artwork" as I also write on mirrors. I know it's sort of weird, but I have to remind myself of what is devastatingly hard for me to accept. The words on my poster are phrases like, "You are not a mistake," "It's okay to take up space," "EAT!" "Hurting yourself is not an option," "God does not abandon," and "Jesus loves me." These words are scattered across this space to coax me into believing I should get up and get my Bible into my hands.

On this day, I purposefully continued from our room past the kitchen into my "holy place," a.k.a. the laundry room, where I have tucked into a small bag a tiny plastic cup and some crackers. I had only experienced communion at church as part of a congregation, but I have learned differently in these seasons of healing. It's also for Jesus and me to have alone. Life is a gift and privilege, so I start by acknowledging this gift and confessing to Him. As I eat the little cracker representing His sacrificed body and drink the juice representing His bloodshed on the cross, I ask Him to please continue to heal my mind and body and thank Him for His faithfulness in this. As I sit on the floor of my "holy room," I am so blessed by the communion, conversation, and healing that transpire there. It gives me the courage to move on to a bite of breakfast, and then another.

It is healing to hand God my mind. Sometimes I want to run away and stop dealing with life as I can see it on tough days; but, in the next moment, I know with all of my heart that I can't and won't. I want to know Jesus as more than just the One who created me, and right now this is how we stay close. Because, you see, He never moved and He has never changed. God's love for me makes me want to take His hand and let Him lead me one step at a time…one meal at a time…through this day.

The mirror above my sink has at least two brief verses written on it with washable marker. Currently it reads, "Trust Me with all of your heart, Stacee, and do not lean on your own understanding; in everything, acknowledge Me, and I will make your path straight" (Prov. 3:5-6). I need His truths, and with verses on my mirror, I begin to see myself differently. It's taking so much trust, and I do get frustrated. Letting go of my "best friend" is scary; but this friendship kills, so I'm out!

Jesus, we need You more than ever right where we are today. Thank you for your faithfulness to us even when we live like we don't want Your help. We acknowledge we are in need of You to save us from ourselves, Father. With You, we are never alone. We praise You and choose You for the help You are eager to give. In Jesus's name we thank You for hope in You and for the promise that You see us as valuable! Thank You, Father!

Love to you,
Stacee

Take Courage

This letter is written by my husband, Doug.

Dear Friend,

I'm so proud of Stacee. In 2 Corinthians 1:3-4, it says, "Praise be to the God and Father of our Lord Jesus Christ, the Father of compassion and the God of all comfort, who comforts us in all our troubles, so that we can comfort those in any trouble with the comfort we ourselves receive from God." It's easy to get lost in all the "comforts" in those two verses, but essentially it's saying that God gives us purpose in our pain. As we experience His hope and healing, He equips us to comfort and encourage others as they hurt and struggle. As fellow journeyers (we definitely haven't arrived yet), we know it's tough when you are stuck in the middle of it (oh, how we know), but there is a purpose for our pain! This purpose, that God would somehow take this story and use it, is what kept Stacee going many days, I think—that and her determination to not quit for our family's sake. And I am so thankful she didn't.

As I stop and think about this journey Stacee and our family are on, I realize I've had a front-row seat to an incredible demonstration of courage as Stacee has walked the long road of recovery. I am fully convinced that battling mental illness, eating disorders, and all kinds of harmful ways we try to deal with pain, takes a tremendous amount of courage. Courage to enter the crucible of change. Courage to do the recovery process—the counseling, the medicine, the doctor visits—in many respects, the courage to relearn how to *walk* emotionally and mentally. Courage to trust the opposite of everything you feel. Courage to face the misunderstanding and judgment. Courage to not quit.

At each step of this journey, I've watched Stacee be courageous. Some weeks, months, and even years, that courage was demonstrated in the determination to not give up, to pick herself up even though she felt defeated, and to take that next step, eat that next bite, or make that next appointment. I've seen her courageously go to church, our daughters' events, and other social events when her feelings and illness screamed for isolation. I have seen her courageously confront the negative thoughts that often "chant inside her head" by reading the Bible, meditating on Scriptures, and embracing Jesus through communion rather than pushing Him away.

All of these efforts, and many, many more, have been vitally important to her recovery process, and every one took courage on a daily basis. Mental illness possesses many cruelties, but I think one of the most sinister is that it not only robs a person of the ability to perceive reality correctly, but it also robs them of the spirit needed to fight something so devastating. It's kind of a double whammy—the brain is sick, and the spirit, passion, and hope that are so critical to help overcome a major disease are gone. It takes courage to do the things necessary to get better, even when all hope feels lost and all you can see is darkness around you. But to those who struggle and to those who love them, God does provide the light of hope. God can and will bring you through this, but it requires courage to trust Him.

The best definition I've ever heard of the word "encourage" simply breaks the word into its two parts: "en" and "courage"—literally "to put courage into." We all need encouragement, infusions of courage, to face head on the struggles and challenges life throws in front of us and onto our backs—especially if those struggles include mental illness.

Allow me to share one vision of the future with you today to "infuse" you with the courage to not quit in your journey through hurt and pain. Recently Stacee and I were talking about some of the negative cycles and patterns in our lives—some we "inherited" and some we developed on our own—and the impact they've had on our lives and our marriage. In the midst of that conversation it struck me, though, that Stacee's determination not to quit has broken those cycles from being passed down to our daughters. Yes, they may have issues they have to face and deal with on their own one day (both from their own choices and the fact that we are far from perfect parents), but cycles and patterns handed down to Stacee are not being handed down to our daughters. The courage to change is going to have a generational impact on our two daughters, our future grandchildren, and generations to come! Stacee's courage, your courage to press on in this recovery journey, is not just impacting you or even your immediate family—you are impacting generations!

There is hope and there is light, if you don't give up on this healing change process God is taking you through! Take courage, take heart, and press on! Trust me, I've seen what courage can do—and it's worth it!

Doug (Stacee's Husband).

The Deeper the Hurt...

Dear Friend,

Perhaps you are wondering, after reading the letter by my sweet husband, Doug, if I get that I have an amazing man by my side—to support and love me, to stand in the gap for me when I've been unable to stand at all. I cannot express my crazy love for him and his loyalty toward me in this life. Each day has been so different, with my mind getting progressively worse for years; but God knew not only that Doug would choose me but that I would be drawn to him. We go together. We fit. He is the buoy in my often turbulent waters, helping me know my life isn't over unless I choose it. I've stopped giving myself that option, though, the more closely I walk with God. Doug is the first person I text when my mind, through Christ's grace, has a victory. His love magnetizes me toward Jesus. Sometimes I ask him how he can love me for who I am, with all we've been through for the last twenty-five years. He jokingly says no one better has come along, so... It's more than a commitment when you do life together and are more than room-mates, quite honestly. God knew that one day, if we continued to weather the storms, our marriage would be more than we could fathom. I love Doug.

Before I continue, one of the most amazing things I need to share with you is that God's hand has always been on my life—for no other reason than I am His, just as you can be if you aren't already. As I write, I try to let you in for a window (no, a doorway) view of things which have transpired in my life as a result of the free will of my family, my friends, and myself. Yes, God is sovereign; but He gives us choices. A relationship with Him is beyond amazing, not by His force, but because of His absolute love and grace. God knew before I was even born that, by the time I was on my own, I would be hesitant to love. He knew trust would be basically obsolete for me because of the repeated rejection I had experienced by the time I reached my upper teens.

I started to "restrict" in many key areas of my life when I was at the end of my senior year of high school. My parents had only been divorced for a few months, and my restricting went beyond not eating much (the beginning of my anorexia). Explaining restricting as I've experienced it is sort of hard, but maybe this picture will help. Think of your hand as being restriction as a whole. The hand is a complete thing, like my life, but it's made up of many interconnected parts. Just as the fingers branch out, so my "restricting" infiltrated into many essential and precious areas of my life. Just as the underlying veins, tendons, and muscles of the hand aren't visible, so "restricting" spreads into less visible but no less present and powerful areas of my life; and these can be the elements that make my problems so obviously manifest and grasped wrongly.

My parents' divorce was devastating for me. They had been married for twenty-five years, and it had been rough for many of those years. I moved to Texas with my mom at the end of my senior year and almost didn't get to graduate. I was lonely, separated from my sister by thousands of miles. This was the fifth move of my high school career and my grades showed it: I cared less about my performance with each new school. After living in middle-class California, my mom and I moved into a low-income area of Dallas. The hardest part wasn't the changed view out our window but not knowing how I was going to take care of my devastated mom. On Sundays, my mom and I made a cake and bought a box of cereal, and those were our groceries for most of the week. Although I knew Jesus lived in my heart, I was scared of how my life was playing out. At that point, I swore I would never be guilty of needing too much of anything.

After school and work, we would walk to a Laundromat to wash clothes if we had enough money to make it worth our energy. I was forming my own opinions about life, about God, and about how I thought He felt about me, due to what I was seeing and living. Abuse from boyfriends was common, whether physical, verbal, or both.

Why do I share this? Because you and I are smart, we have experiences that affect us, and we hurt. At eighteen, all I knew was that more had happened before my eyes than anyone would want to hear me talk about. I was so tired of living. Scared to death of failing at life myself, I was watching my family disintegrate; and I didn't see anyone taking responsibility, so I did. I absolutely did, and the feelings of failure at not being able to keep my family together went all the way to my core. This has been the poison within me for too many toxic years.

I thought not needing, not making more problems, would help things get better faster…maybe. When expressed, hurt can ruin things; but restricting in relationships can make a friend feel untrusted, and it can cause them to go away. Hurt makes food grow in my mouth and my stomach. It has made me doubt things beyond convincing. Like, even the purchase and preparation of food is challenging for me daily. Furthermore, I have, in the past, memorized nutrition labels to convince myself not to eat because the contents of the food will make me take up too much room as a person, a nonrestricting being in this world. The eating disorder can infiltrate the hurt and say, "Don't take up too much room!" "Don't be a burden!" "Hold all of your emotions in so that you are so full that you can't eat food!"

But guess what: the deeper the hurt and need for healing, the deeper the Healer. There are losses here in this life, but there is also the promise of restoration, and amazing gifts you don't choose for yourself because you don't know how. Please accept God's words as absolute truth and check this out: "Fear not, for I have redeemed you; I have called you by name; you are mine. When you pass through the waters, I will be with you; and when you pass through the rivers they will not sweep over you. When you walk through the fire, you will not be burned; the flames will not set you ablaze. For I am the Lord your God…" (Isa. 43:1-3). He's right here. He was there all those years ago when my family didn't make it. He knew who and what I needed and has been a faithful provider even when I didn't stop to say, "God, is this all happening because of me? Are you mad at me? Do you still love me and want me around?"

Today, would you do something I've only done in the last couple of years? Would you go to a quiet place, ask Him how and what He feels about you, and listen to His response? You will absolutely not be disappointed. The Bible says that, in His love, He *sings* over you and me. That's healing.

Jesus, I confess I do not know what I need. I am new at asking for Your divine help and need Your strength both mentally and physically today. I come to You with open hands, surrendering and asking for Your truth to fill me. Thank You for wanting me and having so much joy in providing for my needs. Thank You for never leaving me. In Jesus's name, Amen.

Love to you,
Stacee

The Cutting Truth

Dear Friend,

Because of God's ongoing grace in my life, I get to write to you, and I love this privilege. You didn't just stumble onto this book, even though it may seem like it. With God in control, there are no coincidences. I pray for you, and truly desire to connect with you in any way God lets me. But more importantly, I want so badly to show you through my experiences that Jesus is our solution. He is the Restorer and Healer. I do not know where you are in life, but God the Father does; and I hope so much to encourage you to keep going! Having said this, often God wants me to share things people don't walk around sharing. I've really wrestled with this one. I know I need to "go there" with you—or perhaps with someone you know—as God has consistently kept this on my mind and heart.

One of my biggest temptations is to isolate—to stay out of the way. To stay quiet, unless I'm in a safe place, so I don't later regret what I said. I am not an introvert, but I have kept myself on a very tight leash and, when I have said or done things that aren't okay (in my mind), I have physically hurt myself. This is not something I threatened or used as a cry for help or as a means to manipulate someone. Others haven't known. Self-harm has been a personal thing for me, and a very wrong reaction I never thought I'd speak of until recently, out of necessity.

I've hurt myself as a harsh reminder to stop messing up when I don't understand what's going on or what a person meant or said, and again, letting the enemy beat me up about it to no end. This is a learned behavior, and it is devastating to see and hear of an ever-growing number of others who have adopted this as part of normal life. My self-inflicted consequences do not fit my "offenses"; but I have been in many situations where I faced consequences out of my control, and those have not fit, either. I didn't know this at the time, however. I absolutely did not know that the consequences were too strong for my error. This learned reaction started when I was a young girl, but as I got older, I really believed I deserved to be at least verbally condemned for my mistakes, especially when restricting my food didn't seem to be enough. I've always seemed to have a high pain tolerance. So one afternoon when my husband was in the youth ministry, we received information about a seminar on self-harm. There were pictures on this brochure and in my depression, the images seemed appropriate for me to inflict on myself. Just enough pain to keep me quiet was my initial intention, but my template of ideas of punishment was broadened, and I was sometimes relentless on myself. This, even now, makes me sad.

Not eating helped me "numb out," but when that wasn't enough for me to forget or stop thinking abusive thoughts, I went further in young adulthood, and I have been so ashamed. This has been a tough thing for me to let God heal, and it's been hard to forgive myself. It is, in my opinion, the epitome of self-hate without actually committing suicide. Looking back on this relatively recent memory, I realize I was punishing myself for failing at just being here. I have endlessly apologized for being a mistake, for being a freakish accident, and I try very hard not to do that anymore. Hear me on this, please—God created you and me for big things! He created us *for Himself,* so know that sticking with Jesus, being close to Him, is no dull ride! It's healthy discipline in the midst of amazing love.

One of the most difficult aspects of self-harm to share with you is that it grieves Jesus. If you have asked Him to live in your heart, as I have, He lives in you. My heart is His home, and I have cut, with harmful tools, words of hate on what He created for Himself—not for abuse by my own or anyone else's hands. When our daughters, our precious girls, were little, they would kiss my "ouchies," and I would die on the inside because they saw their mommy's feelings etched on the outside of her body. Words like "loser" and "hate" were written with any sharp "tool" I could get my hands on. It's what and how I felt, and after I would hurt myself, I would feel vindicated—

but only for a moment! The feeling did not last, and I would be devastated, as if a new result could have come from an old behavior. It didn't happen! I just know I've wanted the mental pain to go away so badly I didn't care that I cut; but my tolerance to the pain only grew—and so did my problems. They grew, but God saw my anguish and said, "Choose Me to heal the pain, my sweet girl! Choose Me! I know what you are going through in the mind I created for good things. You can only remember the bad at this moment; but if you will just let Me hold you, I will ease that pain! I am greater, and I love you, though your choices show that you do not know and believe this!" "There is therefore no condemnation for those who are in Christ Jesus" (Rom. 8:1).

Whether you cut, binge, purge, abuse yourself, surround yourself with abusive people, abuse any substance, or have even contemplated or attempted suicide...Jesus wants you to know He loves you. His love is so great that He died on a horrible cross to purchase your rescue out of the depths of sin and failure. So I am asking you to do what I will never, ever regret doing. As I have shared in other letters, I surrendered and came to the end of myself—the end of trying to understand and control my punishment with anything but love from Jesus. My views on self-punishment were/are wrong and complicated. The first Scripture God brought to my heart after my confession of needing His help was this: "Humble yourself, therefore, under God's mighty hand that in due time HE will lift you up. Cast all of your cares on Him because He cares for you" (1 Peter 4:6-7, emphasis mine). *He cares.* He has sat with me on my cold bathroom floor so many times when I desperately wanted to cut words of hate into my body. He knew this, and He helped me see a way that would not lead to more shame. How does this happen? By crying out for God's help, as I know the cutting won't solve anything, and asking Him to show me what He feels about me. I humbly place myself under His authority—not under the enemy's authority, or the weapon in my hand's authority, and not under the authority of my feelings—*God's* authority. Even now, when those thoughts come to my mind, I take them captive and tell them to go away, in Jesus's name!

It takes work to get better. I do not have the energy to ask God over and over why some people recover more quickly from their addictions, behaviors, and feelings. I want to choose to be thankful that I am here and am not alone in my fight. I want to know Jesus more and more. He is becoming that safe place and person I've longed for. I want to choose Him because I love Him beyond the hurt, the pain, the restriction, and the cutting. God knows how this can be accomplished, and He knows I didn't get as sick as I've been in a flash. He also knows it's been quite a journey to get to where I am now. My response today is to obey and let my Father take care of me. My good days are deliberate, no doubt because He is helping me to consciously rely on Him for every single thing. I would not trade this life He is giving me. Our little girls are now not so little. They are precious and merciful young women, and they know their mom does not have it all together; but my utmost prayer is that they are seeing Who does.

Although it's simple, maybe you and I could think of this song today. Love to you!

"Jesus loves me! This I know,
For the Bible tells me so;
Little ones to Him belong;
They are weak, but He is strong."
by Anna B. Warner

Love to you,
Stacee

Where is the Hope?

Dear Friend,

As I write, I am sitting beside a big window in my dining room where I can look out and see pretty little purple, pink, and white flowers. They are small but so strong to withstand the Oklahoma wind. It's a beautiful fall day and the leaves are an indescribable color somewhere in the orange family. I choose to ignore the weeds, because they are just frustrating and ridiculous. However, every time I look, the weeds seem to have moved closer to the window. Creepy! In spite of them, I look out and what I see absolutely reminds me of hope. In my life, hope shows most when my fight is the most difficult, like white chalk on black paper.

Offering you substance does not come from my mind and heart alone—by far! My mind can fail me, not so much in my memory, but in remembering that I have hope. I can lose sight of the many things the Father has carried me through, so recalling a few of them daily gives me an essential accountability that cannot be avoided or discounted. God's faithfulness in my life deserves to be shared because it is real. This is awesome because the enemy wants us to be hope*less*. Let's do this!

I have evidence of God's hope walking around my house, eating all our food, singing, dancing, watching videos online, and TV. I hear hope asking me "Do I look okay?" before meeting up with friends. I see hope sitting on a bed at night spending time with Jesus and sleeping late on Saturday morning after a long week of school and activities. Hope smiles at me across the church sanctuary when I make it to church on Sunday morning—because sometimes I haven't. Hope encourages me to eat so I can feel good and be fully present at an event. My two "hopes" are full of joy and passion about life and for God. I have hope in their imperfections, because they don't evoke the same response within them that mine have created in me I can see hope, and it makes me speechless.

Since God alone can see the big picture of our lives, He knew part of my healing would involve these two precious redheads. Our hope is not in their performance or achievements in this life, but in the truth that there is evidence of Jesus living in and through them. It's a miracle, really. When I see them actively seeking God, I realize that some of the family cycles passed on to me aren't there anymore...and that is hope! To my knowledge, I come from three generations of women struggling with depression on my mom's side of the family alone. My dad's mom also struggled with mental illness. These were amazing women who sought relief to the best of their ability but still suffered and struggled greatly. So when I see my sweet girls thriving, all I can do is thank God for the hope I see, as this cycle of mental anguish releases our family. I have referred to my parents' divorce during my senior year in high school. As I write this, our oldest daughter is a senior; and my mind is flooded with so many memories of my last year at home. Can you imagine my thankfulness that, because of God, her experience does not compare with mine? That's hope! She is okay—full of joy and hope for today and for her future—and her younger sister is following her lead.

I have written about "restricting" in my letters, several times. This way of life gradually seeped in and stole my hope. For years I did not allow myself to hope—all I had to do was look at the path of destruction I was leaving and I was instantly hopeless. If I stop and focus on the people I have lost, the strain sickness and addiction can place on my family and friends, I don't feel good at all. It's too much to take in. My hope is not so temporary most days, but I still have work to do here, with God's direction. So many who have eating disorder and self-harm problems aren't unmotivated or self-absorbed, contrary to what many believe—not at first anyway. We are often overachievers who have grown exhausted and perfectionists who've experienced one too many failures.

Here is where I have to go straight to God's words, or I get overwhelmed with sadness and hope starts to wash away. 1 Peter 5:8-11 serves as both a warning and a reassurance. It states:

> "Be self-controlled and alert. Your enemy the devil prowls around like a roaring lion looking for someone to devour. Resist him, standing firm in the faith because you know that your brothers throughout the world are undergoing the same kind of sufferings." (That part is viciously true... but it gets better!) "And the God of all grace, who called you to his eternal glory in Christ Jesus, after you have suffered a little while, will himself restore you and make you strong, firm and steadfast. To Him be the power forever and ever. Amen."

The struggle is real! Do you want to get better? Whatever your problems may be, do you want to get better? God would never downplay that being here is hard; but His grace and mercy are strong, and therein lies the hope. The enemy wants us to grovel and fail, so anything resembling this is not from God. How different would today be if you and I went to Jesus with our hurt and guilt and fear, rather than to addictions which seek to devour us? Please know, friend, to deny the hope which is truly from God is to literally hand our freedom to the enemy. Hope placed in anyone or anything else is lost.

I often write down what is hurting me and keeping me from accepting hope. I hold the paper in my hands; lift the list up to God, asking Him to take it; and then tear up the papers and throw them away. When I hold things inside, I get worse; so this simple physical act helps me give them to the only One who can heal my heart and make room for a little more hope.

I have a final plea for you today. If you have never asked Jesus to come and live in your broken heart, would you please consider Him? If you have not, this hope (my lifeline) likely seems foreign. This does not have to be so! Jesus says, "Here I am! I stand at the door and knock. If anyone hears my voice and opens the door, I will come in and eat with him, and him with Me" (Rev. 3:20). There is no catch, no judgment, no matter what your life looks like or who you are. For true life and freedom to fight for our lives, Jesus is the key. Wherever in the world you may be as you read this, Jesus translates the same. He died on the cross—a criminal death—for you and me, to pay the penalty our sin (wrongdoing) deserved. That's the truth; and His gift to us is His leadership, love, and forgiveness when we do wrong. I have found that without a relationship with Him, I lose everything. I give Him my life—and there is meaning beyond the next restriction or next cut. Jesus is hope.

Jesus, I don't know where the people who are reading these words are spiritually, but I do care where they are. Choices, patterns of addiction, and the things we buy into can be paralyzingly wrong and not of You. So, Father, thank you for being so willing to meet each of us right where we are, without judgment, and with eager anticipation to give us the hope which is only found in You. If anyone who has read these words of hope does not have a personal relationship with You, I pray in Jesus's name that they will desire You more than anything else in life and invite You to inhabit their heart. In Jesus's name, Amen.

Love to you,
Stacee

Nineteen

Dear Friend,

I sit in the sand, legs drawn to my chest, forehead pressing on my knees, arms wrapped tightly around both legs so I don't feel so lost in this big world...and I think of this road I've been on with the eating disorder. It has truly been longer than any road I could have ever imagined traveling. And although the walls life built aren't as high as they have been in the past, sometimes I have a hard time opening them to let God in. I need Him in. I can hear the roar of the ocean, and I sink down a little more as the tide seeps closer and the sand progressively grows moist. Occasionally, I lift my eyes just above my knees to peek out at the amazing waves rushing confidently toward me. Water, when doing what it is created to do, is beautiful—and so are we.

I am more familiar with obeying the voice of anorexia in my head than the voice of Jesus, and I'm tired of trying to do better, to get better, to *be* better. I want to give up. As I sit in the sand longer, I realize that I don't have to stay balled up in this posture of safety, and I don't have to be ashamed of my progress just because most people will never get it. But I also know I'm not brave enough to heal alone, because that means gaining more weight—and I'm scared to.

I tilt my head to the right...and there He is, sitting next to me. I can feel Him all around me and in my heart. He never leaves and He "gets" me. He totally gets me. I ask Jesus to scoot closer because I hate it when I can't see hope or progress. Because He knows my thoughts and sees my heart, I quickly whisper under my breath "I will do better," fearing He, too, has lost hope in me. But Jesus never ever leaves.

He never leaves. When I shut Him out because I think my addiction should be gone, or because the mental and physical struggles can be so misunderstood—He stays. I can try to be invisible, but

He sees me. But when I am not doing as well as I think I should—with all the eating, my thinking, and being a friend who desperately wants to be a normal—I don't know what to do. Can you identify at all? It doesn't have to be the same struggle or addiction. Whatever you are fighting, where are you?

As we sit together a little longer, He begins to breathe His truth into my life. "Surely goodness and love will follow [you] all the days of [your] life," (Ps. 23:6) and my heart softens a little more toward Him. "I am compassionate and gracious, slow to anger, abounding in love" (Ps. 103:8). He is like no other. "I love those who love me" (Prov. 10:12). I am not alone in this relationship.

For the past seven years, I have worked with a nutritionist to learn the truth about the value in food. I've worked even harder to replace the lies about food with God's truth—lies I had been taught and believed for more years than I can say. It's hard to admit how long I've needed accountability and help with this. But while I cannot choose or control people's responses to my life, secrets are toxic; and living the truth is freedom, even though the road can be rocky. With each lie I have believed about food, there is a memory, so it isn't easy. And while the eating disorder and depression are relentless in their efforts to take my life, my heart is to absolutely live for Jesus at each stage of my recovery—even if some days I start out unable to lift my head as I sit in the sand, so disappointed in myself that I can barely breathe.

So, what does the number nineteen represent? It's the number of actual servings I need to eat in a day to gain any weight. I know. But when I started out, I ate three total items a day, so my body has needed a lot of nutrition to survive, not even counting what it needs to gain muscle and fat. You may be thinking that you would love to eat nineteen things in a day and maybe even then not gain weight; but after all I've shared with you, please think again. In my mind, the number nineteen might as well be the number fifty. Both are just huge. This is a concrete goal my doctors use to help me remember I would have to eat *a lot* for many days to gain weight.

This helps me realistically understand that I can eat and enjoy quite a bit of food and be fine.

In Jesus's love for me, He takes my hand to help me up—it's time to live in His truth and leave the fear alone. As I stand, I keep my head down, which I do a lot in His presence. He takes His strong nail-scarred hand and lifts my head so that we see eye to eye, and says, "Remember, I am the lifter of your head, Stacee" (Ps. 3:3). I love Him. I absolutely love Him. When I am so down and defeated and cruel to myself, it is not because He has taught me to be that way. This actually breaks His heart. My conversations with Jesus may vary from time to time, but I'm so thankful for them. In the past, they did not happen at all. I stayed in the "I'm so done" place of death. Healing has been a process, and so has been my relationship with Jesus. Knowing Jesus has become my ultimate goal, and He wants that for you as well. He is the lifter of our heads, and He will become so much more as we continue to learn and stay the course.

What is your posture toward Jesus right now? Do you have something before you which seems impossible, like my nineteen servings seem to me? My prayer is that you will stand up out of the sand with me and develop this amazing relationship, with one wall at a time going down as you dust off the sand and let Jesus in.

Father, I have so many walls, and I can be so disappointed in myself that I don't want to keep trying to get better. I'm sorry. Thank you for your promises, which you so patiently impart to me when I try to condemn myself in this healing process. I love you and pray for every person who is in a fight far beyond what they can handle. You understand, even if others may not. Please help us not to hide our sickness out of fear and shame but to bring these things to you as our Healer. Thank you for today and for all you have planned for us if we allow you to lift our heads up to see. In Jesus's name, Amen.

Love to you,
Stacee

True Story

Dear Friend,

The following is a true story. I am willing to talk about it now, but it certainly wasn't amusing over twenty years ago!

I had just turned twenty-three, and I was preparing for the most important evening of my life thus far—our wedding. Doug and I were to be married at six o'clock in a gorgeous banquet room on our university campus. It was all lit up with chandeliers, and the colonial windows surrounding the room reflected the bright lights and illuminated their brilliance. A quaint balcony was just large enough to hold the bell choir that would serenade my dad and me as we walked in to the bridal march. The only thing to make the room more beautiful were the calla lilies and berries I had chosen, which would be draped all over the room and complete our wedding attire. I couldn't wait to see it all. Flowers are my favorite. They represent life to me, and although I had seen our seven-layer cake, the flowers were going to be the highlight.

Up a flight of stairs from the banquet room was the bridal suite, filled with the smells of hair spray and perfume and the giggles of my closest friends and female family members. Little flower girls and miniature brides in smaller versions of my cathedral-length wedding gown ran and played, ready to show off their darling curls and dresses. My dress, which once hung on a satin hanger, was now hanging on me [this gives me the impression it was too big, although I understand why you wrote it that way :)] as I was zipped into the layers of satin and my veil was fastened to my red curls. I was marrying the sweetest man I've ever known that night, and I couldn't remember being more at peace and full of excitement—excitement about the present and about our future. My beautiful bridesmaids and I reminisced as we got ready, telling hilarious stories of things we'd gone through as roommates and suite-mates and now as sisters.

I should add here that two nights before, Doug and our grooms-men were playing a few harmless games of basketball to blow off some pre-wedding steam. Doug went up for a rebound and on his way down he collided with another guy's shoulder, breaking his nose horribly. I had barely seen him since the accident, so this injury was my only concern as time was getting very near for me to walk down the aisle to see how he was.

As the final touches were being added to my dress, I received a note from him telling me how he could kiss me to keep his nose from aching worse than it already was, and I suddenly became super nervous. After reading the note, I looked around only to realize that my bridesmaids were no longer around me and that, actually, no one was close by. Then, I noticed my father standing by the stairs. He motioned for me to come to him and I approached him nervously in my puffy gown. He took my hands and looked at me and said, "Honey, I think we should talk about what we *do* have." I replied, "Ummm… what do you mean, Dad? What do we *not* have? Dad, do I still have a groom?" He put one finger almost to my pearl lipstick and said, "Yes, Doug is so ready, but your flowers and bouquets, including the unity candle, are not going to make it for the cere-mony. A friend of yours is almost back here with a bouquet of plastic flowers that you will just have to use. The important things are here, and I know flowers are your favorite, but there are over four hundred people waiting down these stairs and, most importantly, so is Doug." Realizing that people forgive not having flowers at a wedding, but not having cake and punch would be completely unacceptable, I faced the fact with much relief that we wouldn't have an angry mob awaiting us after our ceremony. So, I wiped my tear and got ready to meet my handsome groom.

So much planning and preparation and dreaming can go into special occasions in this life, and still tough things can happen. Of course, now I can see this wasn't too horrible in the grand scheme of things, but at the time it felt so much worse until things were put into perspective. Why do I share this story with you? Because

God has really been talking with me about stopping and taking absolute notice of what I *do* have, and what we can all have. I have so, so much, and I am definitely not an ungrateful person; but I have treated my body pretty badly for so long. So He challenges me to go deeper still. Our lives are full of peaks and valleys, and He has been calling to me to stop—to let Him take the guilt, worry, and regret, which I carry around with me as if I must prove how truly sorry I am for all my mistakes. It weighs me down, hurts me, and punishes me. You see, I have been sick for most of our marriage; and while Doug and I have amazing memories as a couple and family, these memories (if I'm not careful when looking at pictures or listening to stories from the distant and not-so-distant past) are laced with anorexia and deep depression. The enemy wants me to live in the lie that because this is true, this is who I am or will always be—an anorexic and depressed mom, wife, sister, friend, and daughter.

He taunts me with things that are true about my life, but God… God sees me totally differently. He sees progress in my small steps. Again, God sees differently, and I really have to spend a great deal of energy and focus on what God says—even more so during holiday seasons. More remembrances come to mind, more realizations are associated with celebrations, and more pictures are taken to mark the memories. I must be on guard to not sink, and so must you. Please stop for a moment and think about what lies the enemy is hammering you with today. Now, instead of agreeing with the enemy about who we are, let's thank God for where we are right now, because it's the place He is going to rescue us from if we let Him, and we never ever have to come back to this point again. Psalm 103:5 tells how Jesus satisfies our desires with good things so that our youth is renewed like the eagle's. I have lost much time, but He is my restorer. In Jeremiah 32:17-19, we see that the enemy isn't our boss. "O sovereign Lord! You have made the heavens and earth by Your great power. Nothing is too hard for You! You are loving and kind to thousands though children suffer for their parents' sins. You are the great and powerful God, the Lord Almighty. You have all wisdom and do great and mighty miracles."

Jesus is the Truth who kills the lies. The enemy can't have us when we belong to God, so let's fight the enemy when he invades our thoughts. Tell him to go, in Jesus's name! It's easier to agree with what he says, as I have mentioned before, but don't you get tired of what he says to you? It's a brutal way to live...I know. God our Father does not condemn us for the wrongs we have committed. He tells us to take His load and He will take ours. "Come to me, all you who are weary and burdened, and I will give you rest. Take my yoke upon you and learn from me, for I am gentle and humble in heart, and you will find rest for your souls. For my yoke is easy and my burden is light" (Matt. 11:28-30). Only He can truly console our hearts and minds and change us. "You turned my wailing into dancing; you removed my sackcloth and clothed me with joy, that my heart may sing to you and not be silent..." (Ps. 30:11-12). Jesus sees us in a way that we just cannot imagine.

So, how did our wedding ceremony turn out? Beautiful. No flowers miraculously appeared, but it was still such an amazing, God-focused evening. We realized it was just as it was supposed to be. I know that a flowerless wedding doesn't hold a candle to the struggles we go through in fighting to get well. But God, even then, was preparing Doug and me to focus on what we *do* have in Him. It's hard to do...it's so hard. At every stage of my relationship with God, I have needed to be drawn to Him and refocused, especially because of loss soon after our wedding...which I will tell you more about in the following chapters.

This ceremony called life is humbling, challenging, and worth going through with Him, my friends, because you see, with Him, you and I have everything—including flowers. God wants to be our focus because it's then we realize that we can, through Him, wipe the tears away, no matter the situation or addiction. What do we have with Jesus? An eternity with Him. Without Him, the best laid plans aren't ever enough.

Jesus, thank you for loving us. Sometimes You have to stop us in our tracks, pull us aside, to help us focus on what we do have. You are more than enough, and You are the only One who can make things be just as they should be. Thank You that we do not have to listen to or agree with the lies of the enemy. He is not in charge, and we praise You that You are. We celebrate You and Your birth. We honor You by thanking You for how You have carried us to this day for a reason. We confess our utmost need for You and that Your joy, Lord, is our strength. In Jesus's name, Amen.

Love to you,
Stacee

Grace Extended

Dear Friend,

Recently, I sat across the table from a precious friend with whom I have several significant things in common. We didn't have to explain what we felt or meant by what we were sharing, we just knew. You know, the kind of friend that you can almost finish one another's sentences? This gal is my friend for life. It was easy conversation, but our topic was far from that, and I just can't seem to get it off my mind. So my prayer is that God will reveal fresh hope to us in something that is far too familiar to so many…to my precious friend, and to Doug and me.

We had only been married for a little more than a year; Doug was fully into his master's work, we were in the ministry, and I was going full throttle as a new middle school teacher. We were having so much fun with friends who were also just starting out together. Doug and I knew we wanted children, but we didn't want to rush things. We were just getting used to sharing our lives with one another, not to mention sharing a sink. We took the precautions, but…I still got pregnant. Although it was sooner than we had planned, we were so excited, especially with my history of anorexia. Some people cannot get pregnant because of the consequences of the beast; so I was elated to not have that issue, as there had and have been other health consequences to battle as part of my chronic eating disorder.

Our little guy was being watched very closely by sonogram, and as weeks turned into months, my check-ups began to show that he was not very strong. He was, however, still very much alive, and we believed he would get stronger; but I was sternly advised to eat more. I wanted this baby much more than I wanted to deprive my body of food, so my eating began to slightly increase regardless of how I felt about deserving food.

One morning well into my second trimester of pregnancy, I woke up feeling even more exhausted than usual. Our little boy was taking a lot out of me at that point, so I grabbed some breakfast to eat on the way to school. As I got buckled in, I noticed that my tummy was a touch harder to get the seatbelt around; and like any anorexic, I panicked for a moment, but then felt truly relieved that any growth was taking place with our little one. I so badly wanted to be a good mommy even before he was here. To get to my school, I had to drive over one of the highest overpasses in the DFW metroplex, and, that morning, everyone seemed to be headed in the same direction. I'd rather not get lost in the details of the accident, but I was hit by two eighteen-wheeler trucks at the top of the overpass. As my car bounced off the retaining walls, I could see over the railing enough to see the traffic down below. The whole scene was a living nightmare.

As I was rushed to the hospital, I remember lying there in the ambulance with tears rolling into my hair as they tried to get a heartbeat form our son's little heart. To everyone's surprise, the paramedic said we still had a baby. I covered my face with both hands and just cried in relief. That's all I wanted to hear. My injuries included a severely bruised sternum with some internal bleeding, a fracture to my left ankle and my right knee was badly bruised, but we still had a baby! Isn't it amazing that you don't realize how badly you want someone until you don't know if you still have that someone? As a result of my sternum injury, my husband bathed me for the next few weeks because I couldn't sit up on my own. This just made me love him more. His actions reinforced that God chose my husband for me for so many amazing and loving reasons which have slowly unfolded over the last twenty-three years. Please never underestimate the importance of God choosing your spouse or close friends. His wisdom surpasses all we can see or imagine. We don't know the road ahead.

The internal bleeding did not heal like my legs did. So I only got to carry our baby boy for a few more weeks after the accident. The accident was a lot for my body and, coupled with my low weight, this became too much for him. For the next months, this loss was almost too much for our young marriage. I was skinnier than ever, with a cast on one leg, as they wheeled me past my sweet husband to do the first of two surgeries to take our son—so that we could supposedly get some closure and so my body could begin to heal. But I didn't care about healing. I wanted to be a mommy to our baby, and I didn't want to hear that we would need to wait at least a year to even try to have a viable pregnancy. I wanted *this* baby, and for the hurt to go away so that the full magnitude of pain and loss wouldn't have to stay. I had come from hurt, and I wanted to be done with it. I wanted a new and fresh start.

Doug and I...we grieved alone, really. We didn't know how to handle things any other way yet, and it's taken years for us to even talk about this difficult time—even after our little girls came along and defied what specialists said was possible. But I got stronger with the passing of time, and because of God's mercy and sovereignty there was a next pregnancy. We were pretty much scared to death with this at-risk pregnancy, and I had eleven ultrasounds. She arrived on her due date and was perfect. Then, two and a half years later, God brought us through another at-risk pregnancy (with only nine sonograms) to give our oldest little girl a "bestie," and they have been inseparable since day one. God sustained them, and me, and our marriage. He is in the business of healing and restoring. Because of the loss of our precious son, we still dealt with loneliness when we were together, and we felt alone when we were with our friends. I felt like I didn't deserve to be here if our son wasn't; and although time can be a healer, it has been God's mercy in letting us be parents which has trumped the sadness on many days. The enemy has tried to kill me emotionally over this loss, but it has been used by God as a patient tutor to remind us that He has had a plan all along. Even on our darkest days, there is hope when we let God in, okay?

God's mercy and love have given us two healthy and amazing girls who take our breath away. But I want to say that grieving our son's loss does not compromise the thankfulness we celebrate in getting to parent our girls. God knows that one child's life does not delete the pain of another child's death. We have three kiddos in my mind. I have to say this for my own sake. Sometimes keeping this reality in my heart makes his life even more precious. When we see a little boy walking around the church or a restaurant or a store, we seem to stop and watch him wondering if that's how Beau Bennett would look, forgetting he would be almost twenty-two now. We forget this until we see a cute strawberry blond young man walk by; and Doug and I make eye contact with one another, realizing it has hit us simultaneously. But we are okay!

As I share more of my life, please know it is not my goal to identify with everyone in everything on every level. Believe me…I am forever thankful to be able to proclaim that God has not only brought us to this place, but that He will absolutely not leave us here. Life, however, can absolutely be tough! When we live in community, and share our experiences when the timing is right, God allows us to comfort one another—and suddenly there is meaning to our hurt and history.

I am trying to believe this truth: in my weakness, He is not disappointed in me or who I've become or what has happened. In my weakness, He ushers in His strength; and the amount of faith I place in Him helps to determine where He will take me. I don't want to miss out, but my faith can be so weak; so when I am suffering, He often shows me Himself through Scripture. It helps to focus on Him, so I read in Psalm 23:6, "Surely goodness and love will follow me all the days of my life, and I will dwell in the house of the Lord forever," to remind me that He knows we suffer, so we will need His promises to get us through!

Living in hurt and guilt over loss is paralyzing. It will kill us if we focus on it! I am so new at this—and sort of bad at it! I can only live in His grace and can only stand on His promises. He is God. Whether you have had a miscarriage or lost a baby full term or have lost a child at any age, your child matters and is in the company of the ultimate Father. He wants to heal you in your loss. He wants to heal our hearts and help us to breathe deep in His presence. Loss of a child is devastating—and this, God gets.

I have had the blessing of sitting next to so many precious women who have shared about their losses. Maybe if we sat and talked, you would tell me that your story hasn't played out in the way you had so hoped, and you are angry with God about the absence of children in your arms. He can handle your anger, and He can grasp your depth of sadness. But we can't stay in that anger. He sees our hearts, so maybe it would be good to sit with Him and give Him your anger, your guilt (as in my situation), and your sadness. He is the master of meeting us right where we are.

Thank you for letting me share about our son, Beau. Many of you reading this have gone through so much in the effort to be parents and you have experienced loss. I am so sorry. Please believe that when we come to the point of sharing what we have gone through with even one other person, we can heal a little bit more…and you will find it's not so lonely anymore.

I've memorized this brief verse to help me through today…so I hope you will consider memorizing it too. "Show me your ways, O Lord, teach me your paths; guide me in your truth and teach me, for you are God my Savior, AND MY HOPE IS IN YOU ALL DAY LONG" (Ps. 25:4-5, emphasis mine).

Jesus, Thank you that what we go through here on earth is not in vain. You can use anything to draw us close to You if we let You, which is the ultimate purpose of our being here. You know I have been overwhelmed with guilt and sadness for many seasons in the past, about how we lost our son years ago and all of the issues around him not making it. You hurt with us over the loss of a child, and you understand the devastation so well; so, please, meet each of us where we are in our healing. Thank you that loss isn't for nothing, and that You are the ultimate comforter when a life is lost, no matter how brief the life. Bring joy to the darkness of those hurting, please, Father. Thank you for raising the children who can't be here with us. No one is more able. We love You!

Love to you,
Stacee

Light in the Tunnel

Dear Friend,

You know how it is when you have done the same thing for years, and you are trying so hard to stop and do better, but you have setbacks? It can be disheartening. Let's look at two verses, and I have a few things to share to keep us desiring to move forward even on a tough road to recovery—or really, in life.

"One thing I ask of the Lord, this is what I seek: that I may dwell in the house of the Lord all the days of my life, to gaze upon the beauty of the Lord and to seek him in his temple. For in the day of trouble he will keep me safe in his dwelling; he will hide me in the shelter of his tabernacle and set me high upon a rock" (Ps. 27:4-5).

I've been memorizing these two verses. My mind has been giving me more trouble than usual, and Scripture memory is the only way I can escape when my mind feels so full. Thinking about God keeping me safe and protecting me, at times from myself, is more than encouraging—it's amazing, and so is He.

Learning to cope with the mind God has given me—without self-harm—has been more difficult than I could have ever imagined; and a few days ago, God reminded me of a funny memory. When our youngest daughter was in middle school, a good friend who had a boyfriend became "so over him." She just wanted to be friends. After much thought, I'm sure, she went to break up with him. He was surprised she wanted this split, and he asked her why. In her quick confidence she blurted, "It's not me, it's you," and that was it. Now…I don't know the particulars of the situation, but I heard both recovered rather quickly. I have heard people say, "It's not you, it's me," but this was too funny.

I so often want to tell my mind, "It's not me…it's you!" I am grateful to have the mind God has given me, but it is too much for me and sometimes even for my doctors. I've been so tired of the journey lately, and I know I have written mostly from past experiences, but this—this is about the present. My mind and heart seem to heal more and more when I focus on bringing encouragement which can only come from the Lord, so let's continue to strive to get better, looking to the only One who can heal us physically and spiritually.

Growing up, when I reacted wrongly or messed something up, anger came quickly. So when home left me, I continued the cycle. Now, when I am frustrated or upset with myself, those learned responses (now self-inflicted) can no longer be a go-to drug for me, and I can feel lost. Letting God love on me when I do the wrong thing? So foreign. So gracious.

God doesn't react to me like I react to me, and I don't react to others like I do to myself. I don't know...I guess the best way for me to describe my mind would be that it's like I'm looking down a long tunnel. My mind...the way it works and shows me a situation... it's tricky. Some days the tunnel has light streaming through it, and some days it's pitch black. I don't want it to stay black. I never win when it does.

When my sister and I were little, we would take empty paper towel rolls, poke holes in them, and look through one end of the roll. We would cup a hand over the open end of the roll. The light couldn't help but push its way through the holes, and it looked so cool, especially if we poked holes to make a certain design. If we hadn't poked the holes in the tubes, what would the point have been? On the days my mind and heart start out hopeless, the tunnel is dark and without holes. There is light all around me, but until I surrender and let God put the "holes" in the tunnel, I can't see anything hopeful. The enemy wants me to believe there is no way to have hope, to see light coming through, because of the way my mind works. He wants me to cut, or give up writing, or see only the path of destruction I have left behind. In order to bring light into my mind so that I can see hope, I have to cope differently, and it's extremely hard. It requires doing something that, at the time, seems weak and powerless, when I am used to feeling empowered by restricting my food for a few days so that I can't remember. Or it may mean repeating the action of surrendering to God and asking Him to take away my strong desire to punish myself physically so that I won't repeat my mistakes again. It's new for me and I am not all that awesome at it… yet. But I'm not giving up.

It's a waste of life to believe the lies that the world yells at us. It's a waste of life to live as if the enemy is suddenly going to help us instead of hurt us. God is the same yesterday, today, and forever; and life requires obedience to God, who will only guide us to a fulfilling life on earth in order to get better. Although my brain is whole, my mind is divided; and the brain that fights to get better is the same brain which can hear the enemy, which can have endless flashes of vivid memories—both good and bad—and which can believe God is carrying me from the front lines of this battle. But because it's the same brain, it holds out mercy for you as you fight and fail and fight and triumph. Please know that everyone doesn't have to validate the difficulty of this journey you are on. Don't wait to fight until everyone is on board and supportive. When I wake up and can only see darkness, God is ever-present to help. This fight is real, so yes—I do get down, and that's just me being honest with you. I do experience setbacks with anorexia recovery and mental health issues; but God is so big that if I will let Him poke a hole in the darkness of the tunnel, He will fill it with light that can only come from Him.

What does this look like for me? It looks like reading a verse from His Word, the Bible. Then, it looks like letting Jesus give me the courage to get my clothes on one piece at a time, to get ready to go out and meet a friend who may need encouragement, or to get things done at home which help my family. Do not compare yourself to me or anyone else. Comparison can kill us. Learning new ways to survive and live without doing harmful things (including ones I may not have even mentioned) is hard, and God has a personal track for each of us who desires healing. One step at a time, God pokes light into my day, and I never regret venturing out with His help. It's the only way to let go of the behaviors that have worked so hard to kill me. This road, for me, has been over twenty years; and if it keeps me close to Jesus, if the battle reminds me to have mercy for those around me, those God has placed in my life to walk this out with—like you—then I'm in. I'm all in, friend.

"Blessed is he who has regard for the weak: the Lord delivers him in the times of trouble. The Lord will protect him and preserve his life; he will bless him in the land and not surrender him to his foes. The Lord will sustain him on his sickbed and restore him from his bed of illness" (Ps. 41:1-3). I love you and feel the joys and pains of getting better right along with you. You are precious to me, but most important, to Jesus—Who has given His very life to spare yours and mine. Right now, wherever you might be, please let God know you need His help in this fight, to stop using the same harmful coping mechanisms, and to separate yourself from addictive behaviors. Maybe you need help dealing with the discouragement which can come from setbacks in sickness and struggle. I encourage you (and myself) to say to the enemy: "It's not *me*…It's *you*. Now *go* in Jesus's name," and let God show us His light today.

Love to you,
Stacee

Never Invisible

Dear Friend,

I'm sure she was talked about and avoided and, even though others only speculated about what took place in the four walls of her home, they were pretty confident in their conclusions. She was looked down on, her lifestyle and choices were godless. Headed to do what she did each day, she walked barefoot down the dusty road for some fresh water. She could feel the stares of others, even those of former friends, and she came to get what she needed and leave—yet she would have an encounter which would change her life forever. Her needs were greater than she was even aware. Her vicious cycle of poor choices made her look desperate, and she was.

She was starving for attention, but not the type she was getting. As this woman went for water to quench her thirst, Jesus, in His humanness and simultaneous God-ness, met her to offer her a drink from an eternal well that would forever be full. He knew her story... every single detail, and it mattered, but primarily because He had the only way to help her story change direction. You see, until we realize there is a better way to fulfill our needs in this life, it's difficult to admit, or even see, that we need someone to save us from where we are headed, and to get those needs met by the only someone who can...Jesus. Without a realization of our desperate need to be rescued, what Jesus has to offer is a hard sell.

My prayer is that we get to that rock-bottom place where we are *done* with temporary solutions—which only lead to even more destructive ways—and admit our need, which is much too much for anyone or anything on this earth.

The woman I refer to above is a very special lady I have read about my whole life. She is in God's Word to you and to me. His words meet me where I am, even though years ago I had no idea this is where I would be and that my days would have been as they have.

She is referred to as "the woman at the well" in the book of John, and she is my very favorite. Our struggles are not the same, but it hasn't mattered because she is someone I identify with. This story has saved me many nights.

Jesus…He talked to anyone, no matter who was looking. And I'm sure, after He told her He knew about her five husbands and that the man she now had was not her husband, she realized this was no ordinary man. So she accepted what He offered her on that late afternoon. She received His grace, believed in Him, and from then on she would never thirst again.

What makes this story so precious to me is that Jesus knew who she was and offered her what is still offered to you and me today: Himself. Just as He sat with her and had mercy on her, He offers the same to you and me. He addressed her situation of sin, offered her forgiveness, and she accepted and changed. She was one amazing person, and so are you. I may not know you personally, but you are truly amazing. You count and are irreplaceable. But this isn't only my opinion—it's God's. This is hard for me to internalize about myself, and I want so badly to not only take it in, but live in this renewal.

When I am struggling, the last thing I need is encouragement to disappear. I've asked God to help me with this, because at times I have become more afraid to live than I have ever been to die. It takes guts to live. But it takes *God* to live victoriously. After this woman left her meeting with Jesus, I can only imagine the changes which came about in her life. I bet she didn't care what others thought or if they believed she had really changed because, after all, it was *her* encounter with Jesus. I haven't gotten as sick as I've been because I hoped for mediocre. I have passion and drive for a life that matters; and in years past, when I saw and experienced the reactions of people around me when I did something wrong, or didn't do something to a certain standard, I began to lose sight of what was true about me. So lost.

As I take one step at a time in getting to know the truth about how God truly sees me, reprogramming my mind to accept the change He provides, it helps when I think about others He has renewed, especially my kindred spirit from this story about two thousand years ago. I think a little less about what others think of me and am a little less overwhelmed. I care, but caring is different from letting this control me. This frees more and more emotional space to become aware of those who are hurting around me, and I truly believe this is where I get the passionate desire to share and love more deeply.

Love to you,
Stacee

So Much in Common

Dear Friend,

Every real relationship has its ups and its downs…its seasons of distance and difficulty. But if you dare to fight through it, you can come back better, stronger, and closer.

I know in my heart that distancing myself from God was because I didn't know Him, only about Him. I didn't want to hear or face what He might possibly see in me. God absolutely sees and loves and responds to you and me in a way we can never really understand. I thought I knew what He must see, that it must be disappointment and anger and shame—disappointment in me for having mental challenges and for being so full of emotion that I could barely take a bite of food to nourish myself. For years I've felt my struggles were a punishment because of things I've done wrong and how my family finally split up. Maybe if I had been a better kid, student, or youth leader, those things wouldn't have happened. I haven't felt like a victim, I've felt responsible. I didn't want Him to be a part of my recovery anymore because I was angry and tired of trying to get better, and I couldn't see any progress, any noticeable strides. I have journals full of asking God when the anorexia and this game in my mind could be over. Without Him, it's been nothing short of a never-ending nightmare.

That's where I was, and it didn't scare God one bit. He could take my brokenness and turn it into amazing hope no matter how many pieces I have sat on the floor with…I was dead wrong about how He saw me, loved me, and how courageously and selflessly Jesus had given His life for me. The more time I spend with Jesus, the more time I desire to spend with Him. Even now, though, all I have to do is barely turn the knob opening that door to the past, and the rebellion and hurt and fear rush back in with great strength. Even just opening the door a tiny crack can be a setback, so waking up each day and choosing Jesus is life for me.

All of these emotions came back to me recently when I was out getting groceries for our family. Grocery stores are so big and, well, full of wall-to-wall food. I know…brilliant. At times, the grocery store is one of my hardest places to be. I had gotten what our family needed, I hoped, as I stood in the long line to reach the checkout lady who was working so hard to get us through her line. I felt like I'd been shopping for hours, but in reality it hadn't taken near that long. Standing in line, I walked up next to *her*. Our carts were almost parallel and after looking everywhere else, I saw the left side of her face—and she knew it. I looked away and straight down at my feet. I am positive the bruises and marks on her face and neck were not as a result of anything cosmetic she had willingly applied to look pretty. Momentarily, my eyes saw her upper arm, deeply bruised with finger marks perfectly spaced apart— and my heart went from my chest to my throat. I couldn't swallow. My mind immediately flashed to black and white images which quickly dissipated, only to reappear. I didn't want to show my emotion, but how could I stop my heart from breaking for her? Impossible.

Maybe she had chosen the wrong boyfriend or spouse. Maybe he was drunk or she had said the wrong thing to trigger his rage. Maybe someone felt she "deserved" this reaction. Unacceptable. I don't really care about the maybes, because I saw her and I knew her even without knowing her name. She never let even the side of her face be toward me again, and she paid and left quickly. The tears flowed down my cheeks. I couldn't stop them. People saw, and I didn't care what they thought. It's not my responsibility to know the why or how things happen in others' lives before I feel compassion or love. God's got every detail, and He sees what happens in your life and mine, so judgment before love doesn't have to happen.

God imparts grace, not tolerance, to us. He is just, but His greatest attribute is love. And His love is not reserved for when we get to a certain place in our recovery or our lives: it's available the very moment we let Him meet us—just as He did with the lady I wrote to you about, the woman from the well (John 4). Jesus loves the unlovable.

The precious people God has in my life know they could point out my struggles. My struggles aren't easily concealed and hidden. Friends and family could be critical of me and tell me what to eat, because their struggle may be different and they may not get my battle at all. And while they aren't tolerant of what I am faced with daily, they trust God enough to hand me over to Him, and I am changing. They pray with me, and for me, when I cannot pray anymore! This creates change from the inside out—but in His timing, not theirs. It must be very difficult to not try to fix me, and they have cried with me and for me. My family and friends must get angry over the days, the moments, the decisions I have turned over to sickness and addiction; but the greater the unconditional love, the more I want to know this Jesus who has lived in my heart and to see Him as my Father.

Where do the consequences for our actions come in, then? How can others make sure we know we are wrong? I do believe the woman from the grocery store line was very aware of her consequences as she stood there in line with her bread and milk and peroxide and bandages and devastated demeanor. She wanted to be invisible. And I'm positive the woman who Jesus met at the well that day was marred by her sin, and it seeped out of her walk and her talk. And I know that for as long as I have fought anorexia my consequences could be greater, but I have physical reminders intruding on my daily life without fail. God has spared me much, nevertheless.

But there is something else about the woman from the well—about you, me, and the lady at the grocery store. God's Word says this: "Then leaving her water jar, the woman went back to the town and said to the people, 'Come, see a man who told me everything I ever did.'" Jesus told her only a touch of what He knew about her, and He was honest—yet He extended grace to her. Her part was to accept Him, to let Him forgive her and change her. She didn't leave that well thirsty. She left full, not beaten down or abused by their talk. She desired to go and tell everyone Who she had just been with. That's what I desire to do so badly. That's why I write these things to you.

I am still on this dusty road of recovery, but Jesus and my amazing family and friends are cheering me on, so I cannot help telling you about Who I meet daily at the well. I am not ashamed of Him, and His healing is helping me not be ashamed of me. If I give in to my mind (which hurts daily) and refuse to eat, I am silenced. His strength helps me hate what is going on while simultaneously seeing the good and growth in my life.

For years I could keep my hurts all together in one little secret place inside me. I wanted to go through life and look so shiny and not accept the hurts or "go there" emotionally with myself or anyone else, which lasted a total of...not long. You and I—we have things happen and we can sort of get through them and add them to our repertoire of hurts. But please know...they aren't meaningless. If you have shut God out, I ask you to reconsider Him. Even if you did things wrong, if your hurts are negative consequences of your decisions, or if you are a victim of a wrongful act, your hurts are not beyond God. God doesn't make things happen to us so that we will get so worn down we finally choose Him. He does use our life trauma, however, to enable us to see that there must be more. I cannot do this life on my own!

Ask Jesus for help in any way you can. He does not require a formal speech with eloquence. He wants you! The vivid snapshots of the lady from the grocery store still haven't gone from my mind. I wanted it to be me again, not her, if it would mean I could take it from her. I can live through it again. What if she couldn't? I got to my car, put my head on my steering wheel, and the words fell from my lips: "Jesus, come back today! Please...can today be the day?" Hurting for her was the least I could do, realizing she probably got in her car and drove right back to the one who had hurt her. That's what we often do, though. We keep going back for more. Right there is where so much of my daily battle is fought. Without Jesus's help, I go back to the lies and the abuse. It's a vicious cycle. I've been praying for her, for you and for me. We. Need. Jesus. I offer you something and someone different—Him. He changes everything. Only Jesus truly gets the depth of our hurt and can lead us away from the harm.

But looking back on some abusive seasons, I can take them to Him, leave them there at the foot of the cross, and run away without shame to share with you the joy I have today.

Who is this Jesus, who I am describing to you, in your life? The woman at the well—she represents so many of us. She was hurting and her life totally showed it. She arrived at the well not wanting to hear another person's opinion of her life choices, I'm pretty sure. She was in deep need of change, and Jesus became that change. She asked for forgiveness, and she was never the same because she believed Him. She left His presence without shame but with hope—hope for eternity. You are just as amazing as she was, and Jesus waits for the chance to forgive you today, to save you from your toxic tomorrow. Jesus says, "Peace I leave with you; my peace I give you. I do not give to you as the world gives. Do not let your hearts be troubled and do not be afraid" (John 14:27). He is refreshingly incomparable to anyone here on earth.

I cannot thank you enough for letting me share with you as I take each step, and sometimes take a few steps back, in this life. Whether you can identify with the woman who Jesus loved unconditionally at the well, or the woman in the grocery store line who wanted to be invisible, or if you are the friend or family member of someone who only Jesus can transform, please don't give up. Please don't fight alone in fear of what you may think Jesus must believe about your situation. I've only lost ground with my Father out of the equation. You? Me? The woman at the well? The woman at the grocery store? We are all the same. Jesus, then and now—same.

Jesus, thank you for not being shocked by where we are at this moment in our lives. Thank you for being willing and ready to speak with us and be the change in our lives, not the tolerance. You are hope, and I cannot live without you. I pray that each person who reads this will want you so desperately that they will surrender and ask for help from You! In Jesus's name, Amen.

Love to you,
Stacee

You Are Worth Saving

Stacee with her sweet friend Debbie Wallace. Debbie first told Stacee that, "you are worth saving," right before Stacee entered treatment for anorexia. After 24 years of friendship, God continues to use Debbie's words and unconditional love in Stacee's life.

I sat on the back balcony looking out through tall trees. The trees were beautiful, but high and full, so I could only see a short distance. I was discouraged and pretty much disheartened as I thought about my recovery. "You are worth saving, Stace," my precious friend said. I needed those words from someone who knew me and cared about me while I was away for a few days on this much-needed trip. It was late when we concluded our conversation, and I felt safe; then my thoughts changed, and I began picturing Jesus saying those simple words to me. I have them written on my hand often now.

Lately, things had become much more "real" with my eating disorder treatment, thus the reason for the much-needed talk with my dear friend. I don't know…I just hoped I was further along. I was tired, and a different course of treatment had been recommended to me, with great encouragement to get on board. In other words, it was crunch time; and whether I felt tired of this road I've been on or disheartened by my lack of progress, I needed to embrace what I had to do: eat more and pray that my organs will accept and digest the nutrition. Focusing on the truth is definitely where I needed to be mentally, so please, humor me as I work through this. I have learned that the more I share my life, the more determined I am to get better. The more I share Jesus with you, the closer to Him we can all draw.

Our family loves to be in and around the water, with the perk of adding some healthy color to our paper-white selves. I love to watch the tide as it comes and goes in its beautiful strength. The morning after the phone call from this sweet friend, Doug and I went kayaking. While our girls were at youth camp, we had gotten away to Seaside, Florida, a place our family has grown to love. It's our place to play and rest. I wasn't much help with the paddling, but my guy had it all under control. The waves were long and high from the shore all the way to the sandbar. With each wave, the boat lost its place for a moment, but Doug paddled deep to make it past one wave and on to the next. The spray of saltwater felt so refreshing as we went against the flow. I just closed my eyes as my sweet husband got our kayak further and further away from the shore…further and further away from my worries. Closer to God and His creation. I pictured His love and mercies pouring over us as we went against the flow.

Doug has a great rhythm in his paddling, much like I see in his daily life when I think of it. He takes one wave at a time, though not denying there are more waves to come, and fervently prepares for them. Our boat was much too small to be more aggressive. As a wave took us to a new height, we could see the sandbar gradually getting closer and closer; however, from the shore, the sandbar didn't look super far to begin with! To pause in his rowing for more than a moment would mean kissing the shore, so there was no turning back for us! Finally and thankfully, we reached the plateau of the sandbar and the paddle was still.

Going with the current takes very little effort. It's the "against the flow" which can seem so difficult and, without a moment's notice, you can lose the shifting ground you thought you'd passed for sure. I'm not much for the shore, and that's good because my battle is more commonly in the waves. I know I'm not alone in this. When I'm having a hard time getting a clear view of the sandbar, I'm disappointed in where I am. My thoughts of hope can be drowned out, and I can't see what's to come.

When I feel overwhelmed by the talk of needed weight gain and by the enemy trying to stifle my desire to bring hope out of the darkness of each battle, I want to say, "Hey! But wait! I'm afraid of gaining more weight! I'm afraid of all that this means! What if I get too hungry, and I eat too much and feel too much and ask for too much, when I'm more comfortable not taking at all?" See? Do you see why I need Jesus? I get afraid. But when I cannot see where I'm going, Jesus grips my heart and holds me tightly and reminds me that He *sees*. And that, my friend, is when I have to—and you have to—have faith that He is steering us to the sandbar. Believing without seeing: that's faith.

"In my weakness, He is made strong" (2 Cor. 12:10). Friend, He is my only hope—and yours! He is my encouragement and your encouragement. I belong in the water, working this out and relying on Him to show me where to go, even when I can't exactly paddle. Without God and without faith, I'm sunk. But please look at this with me: "Blessed is the man who perseveres under trial, because when he has stood the test, he will receive the crown of life that God has promised to those who love Him" (James 1:12).

I love Him, and I choose to live. This is written on my mirror right now, just in case I forget. He wants me here and knows exactly where I am. He knows the same of you. Please persevere with me.

The enemy yells that I have no place to encourage you because I feel a little waterlogged myself. So, let me encourage you! "*He* who began a good work in you will be faithful to complete it until the day of Christ Jesus" (Phil. 1:6). Jesus isn't the sandbar in the ocean, however. The sandbar is merely a place to rest and reflect. He's the goal, the very Creator of the whole ocean and the sun that shines on the water to give us hope. I am not only looking back on recovery; I'm walking it with you. I am not looking back on the mercy God has had on me; I'm receiving it as we go this road together. I can continue to offer you Him and His ability to sustain and breathe life into us every moment of every day.

Where I am isn't because He is disappointed in me. He runs to me…to you…and shows me more of Him. Whether it is speaking or writing, communication—not silence—has become key to my fight. The struggle at its strongest becomes more faint, and hope becomes more vivid. Waves from the shore are picturesque. Get into the water and live, whatever that may look like in your life today.

"What can wash away my sin? Nothing but the blood of Jesus. What can make me whole again? Nothing but the blood of Jesus. Oh, precious is the flow that makes me white as snow. No other fount I know, nothing but the blood of Jesus." This hymn was written by Robert Lowry.

You are worth saving. I cannot offer you what I wish I could—I wish I could tell you I'm almost finished with my recovery. I want to be one of the 3 percent who is totally well. And I will be. But it will be in God's timing, and that's okay. It's okay because I'm learning what I have never ever been willing to take in: "You are worth saving, Stace." I *am* worth saving, and the verdict can't stay out on that in my mind or in my heart any longer. My body isn't up to the ebb and flow of that decision being based upon how I feel about myself anymore. Those days are over, I am told. The price I pay is getting higher, and the waves are getting higher. I'm not going to ruin anything (except the enemy's schemes to kill me) when I keep fighting to live.

"When you pass through the waters, I will be with you; and when you pass through the rivers, they will not sweep over you. When you walk through the fire, you will not be burned; the flames will not set you ablaze. For I Am the Lord your God" (Isa. 43:2-3).

Jesus! Please carry us, and encourage all who read these words because of You and Your love and mercy and grace. Thank you that nothing I share is based on me being good at getting well. I praise you for where I am right now. I thank you for where the precious ones who are reading these truths are. You are so much more than enough. Thank you for giving us the opportunity to choose faith in You. What a gift! You are our Truth. In Jesus's name give us strength to persevere. Because of You, God, and because You absolutely adore us...we are worth saving, whether we can paddle and row from where we are right now or not. You've got everything under control. Everything. Praise be to You, God. In Your powerful name we thank You, Amen.

Love to you,
Stacee

The Yarn around My Wrist

Dear Friend,

She carefully placed a strand of white yarn in a circular shape on the floor to represent my head. She then asked me to think about my body—about the parts which I felt look significantly different since I'd been nourished during the re-feeding process over the past three months. I chose my upper arms, my stomach, and my legs.

I was then given white yarn to cut and place on the floor to represent the size of those places—the ones I was now seeing as scary and tough to look at in the mirror. "This process will not work if you are not as accurate as you can possibly be. Only cut the yarn the length you think is needed to make the circumference of the size you truly see," my therapist told me. I visualized, cut, and placed the yarn in the proper places, according to how my eyes see my size. It was not a game. The process took me longer than I thought it would as I knelt, recut, readjusted, and stood up only to get a little flustered. This was done with my head therapist, and there is no way I could do this with someone I hadn't learned to trust. I wouldn't have been able to handle as much as a gasp of disappointment or a sarcastic comment.

In her hands was a different color of yarn now. She carefully wrapped it around my upper arm, then cut; around my stomach, and cut; then down to my legs, and cut. She then asked me to place this yarn within or outside of the white yarn already on the floor and, once finished, to stand back and take a look. You know what happened. Each piece of yarn my therapist had cut fit within the yarn I had placed so carefully on the ground. You may think that this showed me how "off" my mind sees my size. You may think that this changed my reality, but I saw the two circles of yarn as exceptionally close to the same circular size. Was my therapist shocked? No. Was I sad to discover that I really can't see this differentiation more clearly? Absolutely.

She placed the longest piece of the white yarn (representing my perception) gently in my hand to keep and put somewhere special to remind me of my skewed vision each time I look at it. I couldn't put it away in the days following that appointment. I tied it around my right wrist. It is symbolic of how much I need God at each point of this path, because I don't see. I need to trust what matters. God sees Christ in me because of His love, and He absolutely does the same for you.

I'm so thankful that He can see.

Anorexia wants to take my life. I went away to learn to reclaim it. Since then I've been practicing, eating, and trying very hard to internalize that God loves me no matter what. This was demonstrated in the daily lives of my team while I was in their care and in my family cheering me on. God loves my new arms and new legs and new stomach. He loves how He carefully formed my heart. I'm trusting He will continue to help me see that I have something to offer because of Him, and not hide in my clothes and try to be invisible…because I desire to share Truth with you. One bite at a time—or maybe for you one cup of alcohol poured down the sink at a time, or laying down one tool used for self-harm at a time. I am learning to put myself back in the present and future of my family, back into the equation of life. It was truly a privilege to have a loving family and friends and amazing care here at home to get me to inpatient treatment.

Writing to you about my time away in these pages, helps my transition so much! Writing has grown into being my intimidating friend that keeps me humble and accountable while delivering joy to my heart.

Consider the yarn. It teaches me daily to surround myself with healthy friends, professionals, and my precious family. They see the truth, while I feel the yarn around my wrist.

"I will not die but live, and will proclaim what the Lord has done" (Ps. 118:17).

The few months I spent at the Laureate Hospital's eating disorders program changed my life and gave me the tools to come home and continue this fight. To learn more about their programs for yourself or a loved one, visit their website at www.saintfrancis.com/laureate-psychiatric-clinic/eatingdisorders.

Love to you,
Stacee

Through Rylee's Eyes

Dear Friend,

This letter is written by Rylee, my youngest daughter.

She's home! As my mom walked through the front door of our new house for the first time, I felt as though there should be a party with the whole world invited! She made it. After what was supposed to be six weeks (which turned into four months) was over, I felt as though the biggest celebration should be thrown! I now realize the hardest part was still to come. I was finally getting used to living with just my dad, and now there was another change. It was a good change, great change…but it was still another change. At that point, I was getting tired of those. I don't know what it's like to have a mom without an eating disorder. Ever since I can remember, my mom has suffered from this mental illness. As I grew up, I hated how it was all a secret. Why couldn't it be talked about? I was not ashamed of my mom, but I was taught by the world that I should be. Few people in our life knew about the eating disorder, which made for little support. That made it even harder at times, but also made us very thankful for the support we had. Too, this helped our family become very close. Now you can see why these past four months were so hard! Our family was so used to being together and in just two days, we were split three different ways.

The four months I was adjusting to having my mom away for treatment and sister, who was at college, were not easy to say the least. As time went on, I realized things were not going to get easier, but that I just had to learn how to handle it. I was told by so many that I was strong and brave, but I couldn't find that in myself. For the first couple of weeks, I would cry almost every night. Where was the strength in that? I kept the feelings inside and tried to handle things on my own. Where is the bravery in that? I realized I could only be brave and strong if I let Jesus in. For a while, I was frustrated with

Him. I didn't understand why on earth He would take my mom away from me. Then, I realized how selfish I was being. My mom would not be able to live her life if she had not left for that time. I could not be more thankful that she received the help she so desperately needed. The Lord was the only way I could have strength and bravery during this time. Whenever people tell me these things, I know it's not me, but Jesus inside of me.

I tend to worry. A lot. Like, a lot a lot. When your mom is sick and you don't know how to help her, it can cause one to worry. Sometimes I just overthink things in my head and then I stress myself out thinking about those things, causing me to worry, and...you get the point. So you can imagine how hard it was for me to trust God the whole time I wasn't with her. I knew she was getting better, but the road to recovery is the bumpiest of all. How could I not be worried? I spent a lot of time struggling because I felt as though no one could fully identify with what I was going through. And then I felt as though God put His hand on my shoulder and I could just feel His presence. He never left me alone. Also during this time, my dad was my rock. We got very close and I feel like our relationship is so much stronger. He was there for me and would listen whenever I needed him to. Nightly phone calls and weekend visits with my sister gave me the encouragement I needed and I hope I did the same for her. Best friends is an understatement for our relationship.

Mental illness has taught me that God gave my mom a different kind of brain. She processes things differently, handles things her best, and feels deeply.

Before my mom had to go to the hospital, things were hard. The summer previous to my mom leaving, she barely had any energy, and her quality of life was decreasing. She was tired most of the time and was weak. Of course, my mom still wanted to do everything with Shelbee and me, which didn't necessarily help. On the inside, she wasn't doing so well either. Her heart was literally shrinking, and she was not getting near enough nutrition. The best thing for her to do was to go to a place where she could recover even if it did mean being away from us for a little while.

Now that she is home, she is happier and brighter. Just when she smiles, you can see life in her eyes! Her hugs are tighter and her heart is stronger. I am so thankful that she is on the road to recovery! My mom is my biggest inspiration. She has never given up hope and is constantly putting her trust in the Lord. I couldn't have asked for a more loving, kind, and strong person to call my mom!

Rylee

My Toughest Place

Dear Friend,

Thank you for being gracious enough to let me share bits of my intensive inpatient eating disorder treatment with you. It has become an integral piece of the puzzle that shows the picture of my life thus far. Today, this letter refers to bravery under pressure.

I shared a table with a group of ladies for several months. I don't know if you've ever gone through a life-changing experience with a group of people, but it is a bonding experience that's difficult to explain because the emotional attachment just *happens*. This is where things got real for me. All of my coping tools were outsmarted, all of my rules were broken, and all of my fears surfaced. And it happened not once, but multiple times a day without fail, because I chose it. But I wasn't alone. Not for a moment.

The brave people I ate around 350 meals with during inpatient treatment deserve a shout-out. They are courageous and loving and selfless. Picture this: ladies going through a line in a small restaurant setting, facing food. Sounds enticing if you love food and aren't afraid of what it will do to you—but all of us are afraid, because of the messages the society crams down our throats. Pictures that have been touched up to make women appear unrealistically thin, life situations that take our appetite away, or the insinuation by commercials that eating their brand of cookies will fill your life with goodness, are lies. Combine that fear with the relentless yelling in our heads, the eating disorder telling us we are weak—giving in if we take a bite of pasta or chicken fried steak or cinnamon roll—and you have the potential for a perfect storm. The possibility of disordered eating in some form.

Why? We go to intensive inpatient treatment to face those fears over and over so that maybe...just maybe...we will discover our fear is an illness, not a reality. But it's not only that. If you are in this level of treatment, the eating disorder is so loud that your health has been greatly compromised and there is a window of time to get nourished.

So we spent a great deal of time eating around a table like most people do—but we hadn't. Facing this fear six times a day was the hardest thing I've ever done. Not getting to carefully control what I put my mouth was emotional—at least for me. I cried through most of my meals, and that's okay because I had professional and peer support. We ate with trained technicians, nutritionists, and therapists. My anxiety was usually at a ten out of ten; but if I wanted to get nourished, this was the deal. The most important parts of getting through each meal, which had been prepared by a chef and staff who cared deeply about the quality of the food and about our recovery, were my peers who sat on either side of me.

Once they reached a certain point of their own care, these ladies were cheerleaders as well as patients, and their mind-set was to go for a level closer to freedom. When being re-fed, I was scared because of my many food rules but, more than that, because my stomach wasn't used to food—and at first it wasn't a welcoming host. I felt pretty bad. But this is why I was away from my family. I absolutely could not do this on my own, and God provided amazing support. My tablemates and I reached a point where we could read each other's outward signs of struggle and extreme stress—a shaking leg, a trembling hand trying to hold on to something as basic as a fork, not picking up a utensil at all...and for me, tears. I never rejected the food. I wanted to show the eating disorder it had taken enough from me, and I was not going to continue to surrender to it, but the tears just flowed.

As we sat there together, progressing through meals at a reasonable pace (which continues to be a struggle for me), the bites would become more delayed. Those around me would begin to talk to me, to remind me of why the struggle was real and why I was going to get through it. "Stace...Doug loves you and wants you to be healthy." "When you eat, you'll get strong enough to go watch Rylee dance and take her to and from school." "Hasn't Shelbee been asking you to come to see her at college and meet her new friends?" "Stacee... when your brain gets fed over time, you will get to write again." There was nothing enabling about my soul sisters. Nothing. With few exceptions these gals *wanted* to get better, and they weren't going to leave me behind.

I miss my peers at every single meal, because we understood each other. Those called to take the brunt of the sickness, anxiety, and the killer in our heads are often in a thankless position. But they see more in us—they see potential in our lives, if we will just choose to take one more bite, and then the next. God foresaw who I would need and most certainly who they would need as we coexisted in this vulnerable position. There were no coincidences.

I am better for knowing them, laughing with them, crying with them, loving on them and them loving on me. God is more than good. He is the giver of all good things. So putting people in our lives, when we just can't struggle alone for one more moment, is Him. At first I felt guilty for needing more than Him. I beat myself up relentlessly for this, but then I was reminded that we are made for community living... and this was the community I needed. The therapists' hugs made me know I could get through this, and hugs from peers didn't let go until we were okay. This was God showing me that survival was within my reach...*our* reach.

You don't have to live in a group like this for four months to be changed to the degree that you can continue to fight a battle. Who surrounds you now? Who reminds you and cheers you on and unconditionally assures you that God isn't going anywhere, that those who love you don't want you to go anywhere? If there is no one, that's my prayer for you—that God will put you in the direct path of those precious people who want you to do more than survive. They won't stop praying and reassuring and loving until you thrive! This, my friends, is why I fight and let others help me do so. Let there come a point in your life where you just want more.

So here's to those who worked, served, and temporarily resided by my side, and to those who prayed for all of the above from home. You are my kindred spirits, my inspirations, my motivators so I could come home to my loves. Ladies…you are so worth saving.

Love to you,
Stacee

Geese, the Pond, and God

Dear Friend,

It was with one finger I pushed the lock button on the passenger door of our car. Doug pushed the unlock button. I pushed the lock button, and he again pressed the unlock button. We repeated this cycle at least five times. There have been several moments in my life that I knew without a doubt I was supposed to do something but simultaneously wanted to full-out sprint in the opposite direction! This was one of those moments. You know, I didn't even put much of anything into my bag for my stay at the treatment center because I was hoping that my willingness to even show upon the hospital campus would in itself demonstrate that I didn't need to be there! It takes tough love, and a lot of it, to get someone in your life the help they need. I was scared, but in my fear I trusted "my love" to help me. I felt so bad physically, and my husband knew this was where I needed to be. It was time.

Each day, from the time I wake up until I lie down to rest, I try to remember what I learned in treatment and act in the present using these new tools. My mind has not caught up with the nutrition my body has received yet. It takes time. My mind rarely calms down, and I am not able to do much activity yet since my return home. It's just not best until my treatment team is confident I can hold steady in my weight range and not "purge" through the abuse of activity. I've said it before, but my reality is that my organs need time to trust me. I have to prove to my body that I am going to continue to feed it. This is my new job and I won't allow myself to quit.

While I was away, the pond was a special place for me. I strolled there often, but my mind-set as I walked was proof of my sickness. Much of my time was spent eating and sitting, and wow, this made the eating disorder angry! Walking was a welcome option, but I had agreed I would limit the time so that my body would keep the nourishment I was receiving. Each time I headed to the pond, I had so many negative thoughts that they still hurt me when I think of them now. "People go to places to lose weight, not to gain weight!" "What am I doing to myself?" "What kind of person doesn't want to eat? I should be grateful to have food!" But one of my most important thoughts from my time at the pond is a memory I don't want to forget, though at times I am afraid I will.

Now, as I have to rest often, I go for walks in my mind instead of physically, and I often head to this pond. I remember the serenity I feel which comes only from being by water. On one particular day, the water was calm...until a family of geese trotted in, and the ripple effect was most disturbing to the glassy view. Cocky little group! But a group nonetheless—they stayed close together. Heading to the water, however, there was a walking path where these birds stopped for a moment and relieve themselves. As I walked around the pond, the remnants of their bathroom break made for tricky footwork. So gross! It wasn't as disgusting if I didn't look down, so I focused on the water and its beauty, and the geese who stuck together, and my walk was amazing.

God grew my thankfulness for the help I was receiving... by the water. God helped me pray specifically for my family and my transition home after being away for months now...by the water. God gave me hope for getting through the next meal...on the path by the water. The geese reminded me that I have support. One major key for my recovery is not to isolate but to use the support in my life as time goes along. I just have to appreciate the sidewalk, as it represents the messiness of where I am while using these new tools... trying to let go of negative and harmful coping mechanisms, and eat. Symbolism at its best. God put it right in front of me for the taking; and when I allow myself to, my mind revisits the pond, the geese— mess and all—and with humility in this vulnerable place I am in... Himself, as my mind connects with His.

As I would sit and walk and sit and think, the answers to those abusive questions began to show up.

"Gaining nutrition is my key to life. Period. I won't survive without it. This is the place to do it."

"What am I doing? Agreeing to do the bravest thing I can: choose life when the anorexia makes me want to die every single day."

"Food? I've always been thankful for food for others, but I could never do enough to deserve putting it in my mouth…until now, as my mind is being retrained."

These dialogues are constant in my mind. Nothing is familiar, though. I am in uncharted territory. But God has everything to offer in His gentleness. He comes and validates that I am doing my very best. And I am more than enough, because *He* is more than enough. Same with you! Same with your battle.

Will you please unlock the door, get out, and let God lead you one step at a time to the pond He has for you…and to Himself? When fear is all you see and feel, I pray that God will help you to stop pushing whatever your "lock button" may be. Life is often messy, and the walk can be messier still; but the water is amazing, and maybe, just maybe, you'll meet a group of cocky geese who will demonstrate the disadvantage of looking down!

Please trust this truth: "But apart from me you can do nothing: that is, nothing of eternal value. My deepest desire for you is that you learn to depend on Me in every situation" (*Jesus Calling*, 261).

Love to you,
Stacee

The Skinny on Shame

Dear Friend,

I just can't thank you enough for sticking it out with me through this walk (or scoot)! I want my sharing to be helpful to you and please know that every time I write it is so helpful for me. I'm in the middle of this great chasm of healing, and I can have such a hard time gaining perspective. I continue to write throughout this time because I know you all can take it and possibly identify.

These feelings of fear as I have committed to eating, and my emotions that feel raw because I am stressed about my new way of life, result in my need to base my trust on hope in God. Having said that, I *want* to be able to tell you my days aren't full of struggles and things I have to work on. That relief may come, but it's just not now. And it's okay! I'm okay. I *want* to be able to tell you that I don't miss the gangliness of my arms which hung at my sides—but I do. Faith and trust come in the moments and spans of time when I ask myself why I have chosen these changes. No one has ever force-fed me, and no one can choose life for me. *I* want to do that.

One day in the treatment center café, practicing just staying at the table even though I was finished eating, I can remember having a familiar feeling—a strong feeling. It was a feeling of shame in eating all that was on my plate, when there were people at the beginning of their treatment at the same table. Through my distorted sight, they appeared to be so much sicker than me, and I wanted to hide. I was a little further along in my treatment, but shame didn't care.

After one particular meal, as soon as we were dismissed to go and wait outside, I hurried through the door and around the corner to an out-of-the-way table. I sank down onto the bench and just buried my face in my hands. I buried my face out of humiliation and betrayal of the anorexia controlling my tired mind. The eating disorder lies and wants to convince me that I wasn't good at anorexia all of those years. Lies. "What am I doing? *What* am I doing?" I kept saying into my hands. A sweet friend and my caring therapist came over to sit with me. Not to sit and solve…just to sit and be with me. That was the day my therapist told me I had reached my nutritional level. This was going to be "me" except for the re-proportioning, which would continue for an undetermined amount of time. (My body would take a different shape over time and I was already intimidated by the possible outcome.) She said, "Don't hide. You're working so hard…Don't hide over here by yourself."

Now that I'm past that actual situation, I feel this is exactly what God is saying. I sometimes want to sit alone and hide in the shame of eating this new meal plan six times a day. But…Shame. Is. Not. Of. God. It's a human thing. Eating is a living life thing, not an action that should result in hiding. I fight this. But as long as you and I are fighting and not giving in to the shame, we are pressing into God's way. Fight in the humility of God's power, not in the belief that God wants to humiliate you. He's not like that. That is not His nature. Check this out: "Humble yourselves, therefore, under God's mighty hand, that He may lift you up in due time. Cast all of your anxiety on Him because He cares for you" (1 Peter 5:6-7).

Dr. Moseman of Laureate Treatment Center has asked many times, rhetorically: "Why does getting better feel so bad?" I couldn't have asked for a better way to express where I can be some days—most days. Why continue then? Because God has a plan for both you and me right where we are. Right now. I don't need to wait for the grand finale of this process to ask Him to use my life.

You and I are on an unpredictable path, but it is not unpredictable to God. His plan can be confusing, with my limited understanding of Him and my inability to fully see who He is making me to be. I am trying to rest in the fact that I will get the "grace for me" truth. It'll come. Here's the deal, though. You and I cannot wait for understanding—we must trust Him to work this out. He will light the path as He needs to. He makes our path to fit us; He's not a part of the "one way fits all" crowd as we move forward and change. At first, trusting God with a struggle feels like jumping off a cliff. But I've found the first jump is the worst, because it's a choice to let go of the controlling best friend who hates you. This is what is so deadly and deceiving about this type of mental illness.

Please don't go to the table of shame and sit alone. Please don't hide. And if that's where you already are, I'm praying for you. I'm praying for people to come and sit with you and remind you of what He sent those friends to tell me: "Don't hide...You are working so hard." Shame and humiliation are not of God. And you are most definitely not alone.

"My hope is built on nothing less than Jesus' blood and righteousness. I dare not trust the sweetest frame but wholly lean on Jesus' name. On Christ, the solid rock, I stand; all other ground is sinking sand, all other ground is sinking sand." Written by Edward Mote.

I did not choose to have an eating disorder, but before I was born and knit together in my mom's womb, God knew I would suffer, and He knows the way out of this. He. Is. Freedom. And the truth is, *not* choosing not to take a bite and swallow it? That, my friend, is sinking sand.

Love to you,
Stacee

Grab the Trunk

Dear Friend,

I often ask myself, if I didn't have the issues of not eating and self-harm and depression, would I be close to God? I'm a pretty independent gal, and God knew I would have an ornery and self-sufficient streak that is far wider than any stripe going down the back of a skunk! I can take no credit for Him choosing me to break the cycles and solid chains of these illnesses in me, to stop these binding issues from continuing in our family. I cannot let that happen. But in the midst of this work, I have to remember that the presence of struggle does not indicate the absence of God. One of the most commonly quoted verses in Scripture is from the book of Psalms, where David writes to us about His relationship with the Lord. He says, "Even though I walk through the valley of the shadow of death, I will fear no evil, for You are with me; Your rod and your staff, they comfort me." (Ps. 23:4). David knew struggle...we know struggle. God's words are timeless.

Look at this with me, though! God knew struggle would be part of our life, so He unmercifully said, "Suck it up!" Actually, that's far from what He said! That's what we sometimes say to one another, or in our minds when we don't understand what others are going through. Instead, the Father says, "In this world you will have trouble. But take heart! I have overcome the world." Hope. Here it comes in the form of peace—peace from God.

Basing our lives on Scripture (not on the lies of our struggles) is solid ground, my friend. And there, in that very spot, is where I am. Putting one toe at a time on ground that doesn't move when I do. Putting my weight on the ground where Jesus firmly stands. Trusting that the eating disorder is *not* solid ground. Even more, trusting that there is life beyond being numbed out from lack of nutrients. The day-in-and-day-out of eating. Fighting the enemy's lies in my mind—telling me food is not for me—with Scriptures. Getting up and making the bed so I won't get back in it. Not comparing myself to where others are in their journey. Not hurting myself out of frustration for eating my meal plan. Feeling angry with my mind because medicine merely takes the edge off of the chemical imbalance. Right now I'm in the trenches.

This is all part of me not merely living…but getting a life—a life of Truth. This will not be my life forever. But each day, for now, it's like I get up and push a repeat button. New behaviors need consistent practice or they are gone. I say the following over and over—I have to or I lose!—once again from the amazing songs of David: "Show me your ways, O Lord, teach me your paths; guide me in your truth and teach me, for you are God my Savior, and my hope is in you all day long" (Ps. 25:5-6). David cried out to God relatively often! He's a good guy to read because his sin, like ours, was great. Yet the Father's forgiveness and hope for his life was greater still.

So to answer my opening question: would I be close to God without these issues? I simply say that there's no doubt I'd be *hopeless* in any life situation, without God literally not letting one of my toes touch the ground apart from His help, His guidance. He is the Healer who mends our hearts, our minds, and our bodies. That's who He is. That's what He does when we let Him, and in the way He sees the best for you and me…and I am growing as a result of the way He has chosen to do this in my life, even when the growth seems slow. Growth is often painful, but how small my faith would be without it!

My precious mom gave me a card recently…at the perfect time. Let these words paint a picture as you read:

"A mighty wind blew night and day.
It stole the oak tree's leaves away.
Then snapped its boughs and pulled its bark
Until the oak was tired and stark.
But still the oak tree held its ground

While other trees fell all around.
The weary wind gave up and spoke,
'How can you still be standing, Oak?'
The oak tree said, 'I know that you
Can break each branch of mine in two,
Carry every leaf away,
Shake my limbs, and make me sway.
But I have roots stretched in the earth,
Growing stronger since my birth,
You'll never touch them, for you see,
They are the deepest part of me. Until today, I wasn't sure
Of just how much I could endure,
But now I've found, with thanks to you,
I'm stronger than I ever knew.'"

"The Oak Tree" (author unknown)

Grab the trunk with me. It's closest to the roots! The wind of addiction or illness or struggle is so strong and many will break under the lies, but God...God is our Father, and our heritage is composed of deep roots. Deep roots! Hang in there with me, please. Let's keep fighting together! We can only endure the relentless winds because of Him.

Love to you,
Stacee

The Truth Is

Dear Friend,

The truth is, recovery is one step forward, two steps back. The truth is, I'm in a tough spot—not an impossible one though. A little disappointed in myself and afraid I'm not working hard enough? Yep. I don't, however, want to glorify this illness by giving it the pleasure of thinking anorexia is going to kill me. As of this writing, I've been home from inpatient treatment for five months, and the anorexia voice barges in in so many loud but deceptive ways. Trusting and believing that God is in control is a discipline, just as eating is. But here's the thing: God is a gentleman and will not force me to give Him control. It's my choice—a choice I face seven times a day when I eat one of my meals, structured snacks, or daily required dessert in order to regain a nourished body. I would be wise to be obedient, to continue releasing control of this familiar territory to Him. Maybe that comes easily for you. But *what* I'm going to eat to fill those seven times per day is a constant surrender...incessant surrender. And God? He isn't disappointed in me. My overwhelmed mind often thinks that He is, because *I* am; but He sees my effort, and He sees yours also. I'm trying to rest in the truth that when looking through God's eyes at this situation, I *do* see hope. Anorexia can't take my hope.

One of the smartest benefits of inpatient treatment is that, during the re-feeding process, I was allowed very limited access to the realities of life outside, but I was not limited in the reality of my eating disorder. We were face to face...head to head...loud mind to mind. This setup is beneficial because if eating is the enemy to anorexia, essential to getting a healthy life, some isolation is essential and, to many, life-saving. It was for me. Removed from that environment, it's more difficult, just as it was difficult getting used to being closed off and allowed minimal outside contact. I think a lot of my time away, still—both the difficulties and the camaraderie of inpatient treatment. I often feel guilty for missing both. This is no reflection on my precious family and friends here at home, but rather a reflection of my mind. My complicated mind came home with me.

The truth is: "Anorexia has the highest mortality rate of any mental illness" according to the National Eating Disorder Association.

The truth is…it's very difficult to share my suffering on this road, but my writings are about the reality of the eating disorder in my life, along with depression and self-harm. My recovery has continued to be a slippery slope. Some days I am so discouraged. I wonder if I trust God enough to continue to heal me, and I fear life without what I have known for over twenty years. Nevertheless, I trust that after all of my sharing with you, you know my heart and trust that I will continue to choose Jesus and His plan for me. Since being home, I only know a handful of people from my community there who continue to stay in recovery. I know people who are symptom-free…but only a handful. In my whole life! And I get disheartened. Symptom-free means staying in one's healthy weight range (as decided by many biological factors), choosing food purposefully over letting the eating disorder choose what you eat (or don't eat), and choosing relationships over the eating disorder rules—the lies set by one's particular eating disorder. By the time you read this, I hope to be back in my weight range. I'm not quite back there yet. I told you…it's a slippery slope, and my mind and body get tired. My heart and mind do desire continued recovery. I *am* working hard, and my body is being merciful, especially considering what it's gone through. I want to make it, to be the next person I know who is symptom-free…in God's timing. I must wait on and trust in Him.

In the meantime, God's view of me and this process is my sanity and sustenance. He does not wait for me to be well or for me to be able to say that I'm one year symptom-free (or even one day!) to help wedge a part of my brain out for me write. He is mercy. He is all-knowing. He is amazing.

Through both success and failure, triumph and torture, David says in the Psalms: "The Lord is compassionate and gracious, slow to anger, abounding in love. He will not always accuse, nor will he harbor his anger forever" (Ps. 103:8-9).

Realize that rare is the day you will encounter a soul who is *not* suffering and struggling. Maybe it is yours. Maybe it's another's. Nevertheless, I pray for you; and God absolutely knows where you are in this time. He sees right past what you may see in yourself. That's good news! That's hope in the tough spot. He is my help to get back in my weight range!

The truth is…sometimes there is no captivating analogy or parallel story I can tell to draw you into this conversation. Life is made of steadfast obedience and it is hard, so I want to leave you with these words that I hum all day many days. It makes my heart sing and the eating disorder furious. Perfect.

The chorus goes like this:
"When you don't move the mountains
I'm needing you to move
When you don't part the waters
I wish I could walk through
When you don't give the answers
As I cry out to you
I will trust, I will trust, I will trust in you."
Written by Lauren Daigle

Love to you,
Stacee

Shelbee's Shield

Dear Friend,

This letter was written by my oldest daughter, Shelbee. I have had anorexia for both of my daughter's whole lives, and would be extremely naive to think and live as if it hasn't absolutely affected each of them in different ways, yet with similar results...God.

My role in my family has always been different. I am the oldest and I have never known my mom without the challenges that come with both anorexia and depression. From a young age, I have learned how to control or in some ways, shut off my emotions. Not allowing myself to feel things or get emotionally involved was a "go to" when it came to the hardships in my home. I felt that if I pretended it didn't happen I would come out unscathed. I remember having the thought, *If I can just keep it together, everything will be okay,* constantly.

I took pride in not feeling hurt or upset with the struggles my family was going through. I had truly convinced myself and I hoped everyone around me, that I had it all together. I actually think I did a pretty good job at it too. I made it my main goal to be okay and I was going to do whatever it took for even my best friends to not know what was really going on in my life.

Whenever my mom went to treatment for anorexia, I was affected in a different way than the rest of my family. I was starting the first semester of my freshman year of college, and my life was full of distractions. I was in a new city with new people and had none of the comforts of my old life and on top of that I knew my family was struggling at home. I was tired of constantly faking it. I was tired of people not truly knowing me because I wouldn't let them. I remember one night sitting on my bed, writing in my prayer journal and being completely overwhelmed with where my life was at. I had nothing to cling to.

That was a turning point for me. That was the first time I realized that I do not need the comforts that this world provides. All that I need to be okay is Jesus. Plain and simple. I had the great joy and hardship of truly experiencing that. All I had was Jesus and that was all I needed. He was the only constant in my life, the only thing I had to rely on and I was okay. Looking back, I realize that I grew in my relationship with the Lord in so many ways during that time. When I was searching for Him, He was present. When I was lonely, He provided friends. When I was down, He provided encouragement. When I needed guidance, He provided passages and verses. "Let them give thanks to the Lord for his unfailing love and his wonderful deeds for mankind, for he satisfies the thirsty and fills the hungry with good things" (Ps. 107:8-9).

Through this time in my life of learning to find my comfort and identity in Jesus alone, I have desired to grow in other ways as well. I am learning that emotions are okay and not a weakness, being vulnerable with others is a way to grow relationships not end them, and when you put all of your hope in Jesus Christ you will not be disappointed. I am continually encouraged by Lamentations 3:22-23, "Because of the Lord's great love we are not consumed, for his compassions never fail. They are new every morning; great is your faithfulness." He is enough for me and He is enough for you. I do not need anything else.

Shelbee

These Seven Words

Dear Friend,

Please bear with me as I share a story so close to my heart, that I know it has become a part of the very fiber of who I have become. I hope it reaches your soul wherever you might be on your path of this life.

My little feet shifted in my shoes as I walked up one stair, then two…three steps, then four. There were endless stairs leading up to the school I attended in first grade. The building sat on a large hill, and to finally reach the front doors seemed like more of a commitment than I wanted to agree to. I didn't want to go to school. I mean, I had friends, liked my teacher, and liked to learn; but going meant leaving my parents. There were problems at home.

Kids don't miss a thing. Their perception of the world around them is broad and hopeful. No matter what is going on in the walls of their house, however, it's my conviction and experience that they will protect the ones who they call mom and dad to the bitter end—or at least one of them—no matter what.

I don't write about my childhood as a rule, but this time it's for a reason that brings about an important lesson. God blessed me with two hard-working parents and I have always adored them. My heart is to bring them respect and let God have the glory for the few things I will say in order to help me get the point across.

I didn't just walk up the steps of my school. It was with careful intention that I took each stair. I wanted to stay home, because I thought if I stayed home I'd be able to make things better; and if I was away, things wouldn't go so well. Every home has its problems and obstacles, but I wanted to fix ours so I could go to school and not be worried. My stomach hurt every morning, and I knew why—and so did my mom and dad. I just wanted things to be good…happy… stable. Obviously, I had to go to school. I had missed the maximum amount of days already, so my mom taught me words that were more than just that—simple words that gain deeper meaning with each year I grow older. These words pointed me to God, not my situation…not my fears.

Before I got out of the car, tears and long wet strands of red hair covering my face, there were a few final pleas with my mom to let me go back home with her, to help her do chores and visit. "I'll be extra good and we'll have fun!" I'd say, to no avail at this point—my mom couldn't give in. She knew it was best for me to go up the hill and learn. She would wipe my eyes with a cotton cloth and re-barrette my hair. I remember our ritual as if it were this morning. It went something like this: "Stacee, remember that God never goes away. You can trust Him when you feel like everything else is all messed up. Remember what to say with each stair as you walk up to school." I'd hug her so tightly, as if I wasn't going to see her again in a few hours, and start to move away. "I trust you, Lord, I trust you." Next set of steps. "I trust you, Lord, I trust you." All the way up to the top, this is what I'd repeat—sometimes in my head, and sometimes in a whisper.

This is what it took to get me into school, and now to do life, though it sounds exhausting to even read about. I'm sure it was more exhausting for my mom to go through each morning. But we knew it was more than that, and it worked because God was and is in it— and His ways work. This, He promises. God has used these words to carry me from first grade through twelfth grade, college, my parents' divorce, my parents remarrying new spouses, twenty-three (update?) years of marriage to my husband, the loss of our son, the birth of our two healthy girls, continuing to raise our girls, ministry, psychiatric treatment, eating disorder treatment, daily chemical depression, daily celebrations for eating and fighting the depression, celebrating the little things, and so much more. These words are what take the pressure off me and transfer the trust to the only One who absolutely never worries.

The sooner we practice transferring our trust from people or our situation and look to God, the better. This is so hard! We can *see* people, their faces, their help. But look at Jesus's record! Jesus never fails, and we can experience his love and other perfections to their fullest day after day—especially His peace. When I start to doubt, it's time to go straight to His Word. Look at this:

"Your word is a lamp unto my feet and a light unto my path" (Ps. 119:105).

"Trust in the Lord with all of your heart and lean not on your own understanding; In all your ways acknowledge Him and He will make your path straight" (Prov. 3:5).

Our lives are full of challenging steps, my friends. This we all know. We've got to choose to trust Him as we climb one stair, then the next. Some of the toughest lessons occur when we are scared to let go instead of trying to stay and fix things. Let's trust that *not* focusing on our situations will be the best option, because one of God's greatest desires is for us to transfer our trust to Him, saying and living by the words my mom taught me: "I trust you, Lord, I trust You." Not only might you say it in your head and possibly even whisper it, but you could dare to believe it.

Love to you,
Stacee

Valley Girl

Dear friend,

My prayer is that this letter finds you well as we learn to rest in our Father's strong arms.

"Rest snugly in My everlasting arms. I do not despise your weakness, My child. Actually, it draws Me closer to you, because weakness stirs up My compassion—My yearning to help. Accept yourself in your weariness, knowing that I understand how difficult your journey has been. Do not compare yourself with others who seem to skip along life-path with ease." "I have gifted you with fragility providing opportunities for your spirit to blossom in My Presence" (Sarah Young, *Jesus Calling,* page 235).

It's precious to God for you and me to need Him.

Although I have lived in Cali, I'm not the kind of "valley girl" you may be thinking of. God keeps me close because I am so quick to try the self-sufficient game. So, let me ask you…can you remember a time when your situation felt so grim that you truly felt like there was no way God could be near? Is that time now? Maybe you've had one trial after another, almost to the point of embarrassment. I get it…thus the opening quote! We are going to be okay, though! I believe this because of the truth in these words from Isaiah 54:10: "'Though the mountains be shaken and the hills be removed, yet my unfailing love for you will not be shaken nor my covenant of peace be removed,' says the Lord, who has compassion on you."

When the mountains are shaken in our lives, and you and I know we are not living on a mountaintop, our hearts can feel like they're in a valley. A low place. Let me tell you something about the valley, though: being in the valley doesn't mean you are disobeying God and therefore you don't get to be with those on high. Valleys have creeks to walk in until we get stronger; streams to drink from that help us regain our health; and trees to practice climbing through to see the truth. Valleys are God-made practice grounds for us to grow until He places us on the mountaintop to glory in His victory.

I have found myself to be primarily a "valley girl." It's not on purpose, but I have noticed that even though mountains, when climbed to the top, are amazing and beautiful, the journey through the valley is where the lessons are. There, weakness is a good thing; the path you and I have been on is treated carefully and validated as being flat-out hard; and God in His utter compassion draws near. When I am on the mountaintop and my mind isn't hurting with depression, and my bites of food aren't as difficult, strangely enough, I miss the valley. In my weakness, He is made strong, and it's all about Him. I. Like. That.

If you and I are *never* in the depth of the valley, learning and growing closer to our Father, we won't appreciate the mountain and all of its views. God is in both places.

Are you in the valley? Please don't be embarrassed. There is no shame in being teachable. When I compare my journey to another's, I'm doubting that God has my very best interest at heart. God is the lifter of our heads…In our fragile states, He teaches us to long for our spirits to blossom in His presence. This He wants to share with us! God is not a bully pushing us further down into the ground. And there is no shame, my friend, in being a "valley girl" when God is working His way in my life—and yours!

Father God, thank you for using valleys to teach us obedience and make us strong for the journey to come. You know what each of us needs. Thank you that any place with you is worth the stay until you move us to the next place. Thank you that when we are in your care we have no reason to be embarrassed about where you have us. Please show us how to accept your help, your love, and your compassion as the gifts You made them to be. In Jesus's name…Amen.

Love to you,
Stacee

Relentless

Dear Friend,

How are you today? I hope that by the conclusion of the letter to you, that you will feel loved and rejuvenated with me!

He left His Father and perfect home to come down to earth. He healed people, He sat with those no one sat with, and He forgave. He was misunderstood, judged, sentenced to death on a rugged and heavy cross. He died on that cross after a brutal beating, and He did not blame you or me. He knew what our sins would be, and He still rose again. He still loves us and seeks after us. This is what I call relentless. This is Jesus.

According to *Webster's Dictionary*, the word "relentless" is an adjective meaning to show intensity and strength, unrelenting. It is persistent, constant, nonstop, endless. This is the description of God's love for you—and for me—and no one knows us better.

God is persistent in His pursuit for the hearts of His people. He is actively, tirelessly working in our world to seek and to save those who are lost. He never grows weary of being the only hope that is unshakeable.

Nevertheless, this word did not initially come to my mind today in the context I just shared with you. I'd been making beds, putting stuffed animals in their specific spots, fluffing pillows, and listening to the enemy. He was yelling in my head about how disappointed God must be in me and my life; and, without knowing God, I would have easily agreed with his lies. It's awful, though! God never intended this kind of relentlessness for anyone, and yet the enemy schemes like this in many lives.

As I sit with and listen to others, I realize this relentless emotional abuse from the enemy can be status quo. I want, more than anything, to experience God in the way He intends, because He is intense about us—and I'm getting there. But I can be relentless toward myself; and the truth is, I can forgive others of their negativity toward me and yet not forgive myself. It's a tough way to go about the day, isn't it? And yet many of you can identify, if you are honest with yourself and with God.

I forget that God is not disappointed in me for struggling. I forget that nothing can separate me from His love. I forget that He died for me, too, knowing I was going to hurt through an eating disorder that is so controversial and depression that is so conflicting. It can be devastating—and yet God does not leave. He is anything but confused about who I am in Him.

When Jesus came to earth He was fully God and fully man. He had the same temptations we experience, but He did not sin. He also knew that, given the same situations, we *would* sin. The fact is, we need to know that He has gone through pain, joy, anguish, laughter, love, and death here on this earth in order for us to trust Him...to identify with Him. If He hadn't, we would've said that He just doesn't understand what we face, what we experience. Because of our sin here on earth, we need His forgiveness. Forgiveness takes down the wall between Him and us and builds a wall between the enemy and us so that there is peace and life. Jesus's death on the cross is our life. Because He rose again on the third day, we serve a living and breathing God who is relentlessly seeking relationship with us.

So...when the enemy is yelling at us, what's the plan? Go to where Jesus is. He is on the high road, and we are to join Him there. The other path leads to sin and death. But He is eternal life! "I have called you to live ever so closely with Me, soaking in My presence, living in My peace." (Sarah Young, *Jesus Calling*, page 175). Don't you want that? I do, but a life of turbulence feels so much more deserved and therefore comfortable. This should not be! As a follower of my living God, I always need to be on a different path, to go wherever He leads. This is relentless living! The opposite of relentless is apathetic and lazy—letting the enemy yell in my head and agreeing with him.

Letting Jesus set the pace is trust. God's Word goes like this: "'For I know the plans I have for you,' declares the Lord, 'plans to prosper you and not to harm you, plans to give you a hope and a future.'" Readers usually stop there, but check out what comes next: the Lord says, "Then you will call upon me and come and pray to me, and I will listen to you. You will seek me and find me when you seek me with all you heart. I will be found by you." Jeremiah writes this in chapter 29:11-14. This is relentless living!

Please join me in seeing the meaning of this word "relentless" as God intends it to be: seeking the truth without end and not accepting the lies that seep in during quiet alone moments. That, my friend, is a step closer in obedience. This is purposeful living which cultivates endless hope!

Love to you,
Stacee

Be Still, My Heart

Dear Friend,

I was walking back from one of my college classes, my hair and dress blew in the wind. Our alma mater sits on a hill in Dallas…a very windy hill! Up the ramp I started when I heard a familiar voice: "Stacee! Wait up!" It was my good friend, who I had known for just over three years. We were in the same group of friends, so I saw him pretty often. When I stopped and he caught up to me, I quickly noticed that his lips looked particularly white, and his ears were bright red. Weird. He started to talk about random things—the weather, how he liked my dress—and then it came out. "Would you go with me on the hayride and bonfire coming up?" I quickly said yes and dashed up the ramp toward my dorm. Be still, my heart!

I ran into my room, flung myself onto my unmade bed, and started telling my roommates that Doug Goetzinger had just asked me out! I remember talking louder and louder as my excitement grew. Everybody loved Doug—everybody. He had the reputation of being good to his dates; he was just one of those guys who everyone called forever friend (this is still true). He was *my* date, and I was excited to be asked by such a good guy. Well, that was our first flirty encounter, and they've not really ever stopped. Twenty-three years later, I can say we've definitely had our struggles; but in spite of this, "Be still, my heart!" is still my soul's reaction. My guy takes such good care of me…and of our girls. I am thankful to call him my husband…my best friend…my partner in crime.

But this relationship hasn't just happened! Trust me! As I've stated, there have been peaks and valleys. There have been moments of devastation and moments of jubilation. Sometimes we wondered if joy would come in the morning.

Picture this with me…A man drives to work, expecting a busy morning. He's running particularly late and is bothered that he had to leave home without loving on his family before the day began. As he gets out of his car and heads up the stairs to his office, he hears a familiar voice calling to him. He pauses, but then resumes his quick pace until he hears the call again. "Wait up!" He stops mid-step, slightly annoyed with himself. Quiet words meet his ears. It is his Father, beckoning with clearer speech than humanly possible. "Would you like to spend your day with me? I mean, you obviously need to work, but can I be your motivation and encouragement and integrity? Would you dare to answer colleagues with grace because of my grace demonstrated toward you?" He answers, "Yes, Lord!" and runs up the stairs and into his office.

He flings himself into his chair, telling his assistant that God had just asked to be a part of his day. As he talks, his voice gets louder—he is grateful that he stopped on the steps so that Jesus could talk with him. Be still this gentleman's heart!

Not everybody loves God. He has a different reputation with those who truly know Him than with those who absolutely do not. His Son Jesus is the greatest man, who only some call Savior. He takes incomparable care of His people and I am privileged to call Him my God...my Healer...my Rescuer.

But this relationship does not just happen! Trust me! There have been peaks and valleys. There have been moments where I've felt crushed and moments of jubilation, but all the while God the Father has been in control. Joy, with Him, *always* comes in the morning.

God wants us to love Him and seek Him so that when He speaks to us, it melts our hearts to the point of obedience. When we stop, listen, and obey, His heart is full, and so are ours.

When we experience God, can our souls say, "Be still, my heart?" Why does He have to call out to us? Read this word picture of just how God works: "Here I am! I stand at the door and knock. If anyone hears my voice and lets me in, I will come in and eat with him and him with me" (Rev. 3:20). He is so lovely to wait for us, but it's our return action that shows obedience. Your answer...my answer turns the knob and opens the door to God for more than a date.

It's not far-fetched to be excited for and anticipatory of God's call. I was so excited about my date with Doug—and that's great and natural. But imagine this: imagine bringing that joy to the door as we let Jesus in to sit with us, to guide our days, to forgive us of sin in our relationship. Let's get excited about this relationship with Jesus, whether it be an old relationship or new. Let us be quick to say, "Yes, Lord!" as we run through our days. Share the good news of Jesus. Get close enough to Him Who formed our hearts, and say as He calls to us: "Be still, my heart!"

Love to you,
Stacee

Highly Unlikely

Dear Friend,

Grab your coffee, and I'll grab my Diet Coke, and let's sit together for just a few minutes. Part of living in community is sharing what's on our hearts, which is a joy of mine that, as long as I'm given the privilege, I will love so much. I care about you and want to use God's truth, not my interpretation of it, to gain God's perspective on you and on me.

David, who was a young shepherd boy, defeated a literal giant named Goliath. He found favor in the eyes of God and became a great king with many problems (lust being one). Nevertheless, He was chosen by God—although he still suffered consequences from his actions. If you had known him, you might've thought he had too many issues to lead a country in mighty ways. He was a great leader only because of God's mercy in his life and by the power of the Holy Spirit. David was a man who seemed *highly unlikely* to be used by God, but he was—in incredible ways—because of the Lord.

Peter, Thomas, Judas, and Matthew were just a few of Jesus disciples. Man, they were different! It's easy to think of them as being so holy because they were Jesus chosen understudies. Peter talked too much and just couldn't seem to keep his foot out of his mouth. Thomas doubted Jesus even after seeing His power demonstrated time after time through miracles—miracles we choose to believe in faith since we weren't there to see. Then there was Judas. You know him, he voted for Jesus to be crucified, yet he knew Him personally. On the eve of Jesus crucifixion, Peter denied Him three different times, just as Jesus had foretold. Devastating, yet I can identify with each of these men and so many others, including women of the Bible. Can you allow yourself to identify with any of these people? It's humbling to do so yet necessary to learn and grow. Levi was a businessman, chosen by Jesus to follow Him and later renamed by

Him. We call him Matthew. He didn't bear the title "minister," but that didn't matter. These were random people who were put together to fit together and follow, men who were *highly unlikely* to be chosen…yet they were.

God is in the business of using those others may overlook, or judge, or cast aside. I am the wife of a former minister, and I have extreme difficulty putting food into my mouth in order to nourish the body God gave me. It's a sickness, a mental illness. I didn't plan it or merely want to be skinny and so stopped eating. That's simply not how it worked for me. I wake up in the morning praying and never say "Amen" until I lie down at night; yet the chemical imbalance in my mind creates depression, so I can be down when I have the best life I could ever ask for. Some side effects of my medication have hurt my body, and I have hurt my body by choice because I have felt I deserved the pain. Wrong. And yet Jesus looks on me and lives in me and has mercy on me. He lets me speak into your life because I love Him and want to follow Him and obey Him and show you Him so that you, too, can experience His love and forgiveness. I am trying! A friend recently sent me this quote: "I am strong, but I am tired." (Brenda Joyce) God knows you and I get tired of who we are, what we do, and the hurts our issues cause. Perhaps by man's standards I am *highly unlikely* to be used by Him, but He uses you to give me hope because you read these pages and share your hearts with others, and I thank you. The praise and credit is God's. When we let Him, our Father uses our weaknesses to show His strength.

You may feel so insignificant you can barely breathe. I understand, my friend. So does our Lord.

God makes beauty from ashes. You know this because I've referred to this truth before. It's Scripture. It's okay to acknowledge where you are. You must, in order to realize how precious God is. Today, read this familiar word from God aloud with me: "For you created my inmost being; you knit me together in my mother's womb. I praise you because I am fearfully and wonderfully made; your works are wonderful, I know this full well. My frame was not hidden from you when I was made in the secret place. When I was woven together in the depths of the earth, your eyes saw my unformed body. All the days ordained for me were written in your book before one of them came to be" (Ps. 139:13-16).

No one who makes a difference in the eyes of God does so because of who they are.

He knew this of David…of Peter…of Thomas…of you and of me; and in His eyes, you and I are actually *highly likely* because of Him alone. You and I? We are the righteousness of Christ!

Jesus himself is the best example of being an unlikely candidate to hold any power or attention here on earth; yet it makes me cry to think of how He came, He lived, he died, and He rose. To those here on earth, He fit no stereotype of the King—yet He was. Highly unlikely? Most definitely—that is, to everyone but His Father…and He is the only One who matters.

No matter what you have done or had planned to do, let God treat you as you were created to be treated—in spite of you, and because of Him. It's okay! Lean in on Him, my chosen friend, and walk in truth: you are *likely* to speak into another's life. *Likely* to have integrity in the life God has given you. *Likely* to thrive because of Him. Don't wait to feel worthy. Come to Him now…just as you are.

Love to you,
Stacee

What I Want You to Know

Dear Friend,

This is probably weird, but I am forever writing notes on topics God gives me to share. It's not uncommon for me to write these ideas on my hands, gum wrappers, receipts, napkins—the list goes on! I can be in a movie or at my kitchen table praying, and I'll have to start writing as soon as I can get to my computer so that I can share my heart. God means for us to draw near to Him and sometimes to huddle together and learn in the midst of our problems and trials. We teach one another.

I am frequently asked what it's like to have anorexia, to fear the effects of the very sustenance which keeps me alive…the very thing God made to nourish me. It is so hard to explain, and I often fumble over my words when trying to describe a meal or day to someone. Though I live it, so many don't, and they struggle to understand the fact that eating disorders seek to end lives. I've never been "called" to convince others that this mental illness exists. I don't have the energy to, quite honestly. But I do believe God has called me to inform you about what I have learned and am living. I am one who knows eating disorder and chemical depression, and I know the path He has me on to healing.

My youngest daughter showed me a list of things which I believe are very true about eating disorders. Unfabricated yet not understated truths. I know you deal with such important things, my friend, and sometimes there is a gap in understanding when we so badly want to *get* each other. It's less lonely in our community when we gain knowledge and truth about one another. Having prefaced this information with my heart's desire, here are *Nine Truths about Eating Disorders That May Surprise You*, according to the National Eating Disorder Association from early 2015. Knowledge is power, so let's look at these facts.

Truth No. 1: Many people with eating disorders look healthy, yet may be extremely ill.

Truth No. 2: Families are not to blame and can be patients' and providers' best allies in treatment.

Truth No. 3: An eating disorder diagnosis is a health crisis that disrupts personal and family functioning.

Truth No. 4: Eating Disorders are not choices, but serious biologically influenced illnesses.

Truth No. 5: Eating Disorders affect people of all genders, ages, races, ethnicities, body shapes, and weight, sexual orientations, and socioeconomic statuses.

Truth No. 6: Eating Disorders carry an increased risk for suicide and medical complications.

Truth No. 7: Genes and environment play important roles in the development of eating disorders.

Truth No. 8: Genes alone do not predict who will develop eating disorders.

Truth No. 9: Full recovery from an eating disorder is possible. Early detection and intervention are important.

Without knowledge, it's so easy to miss-speak. We *intend* to speak in love, so give others the benefit of the doubt and know their hearts mean well. So, what do we say? None of us fully knows the magnitude of another's struggle; but I can speak to what I've been asked, as one who has been in inpatient eating disorder treatment and inpatient treatment for depression. With both, consider asking how the person is *that day*. Fighting a battle is one moment, one day at a time…nothing more. More is too much. Tell them how courageous they are for fighting their battle.

With eating issues, try to steer clear of comments about external appearance. It's too sensitive—the person wants to believe they have more to offer than their appearance, especially if they have had to gain weight and then live in a society that desperately strives to lose weight. Some anorexics and bulimics will never get to exercise again after treatment and the re-feeding process. Moderation just seems impossible, so exercise abuse is common. Therefore, exercise is often not a part of life for someone with this history. It's tough! Putting on "nutrition," feeling like this new body is foreign, then knowing you can't handle moderate exercise to tone the new body, is stressful at the very least. At times, even limited exercise is one of the reasons for relapse. Sometimes the body has just undergone too much abuse. This is my current reality. So again, to an eating disorder patient, physical comments usually send a different message than was intended; and you as their friend will not be able to dig them out of the emotional spiral triggered by your innocent words. Man. It's tough, isn't it? We all mean so well, but sickness makes words translate differently. My mind easily gets lost in translation. Be patient! Your words can be like a healing balm with just a little guidance from those God puts in your life, and from God Himself. He always says the right words.

Even more common than the eating disorder is depression. Words of godly affirmation may not seem to be received well, but I promise you that it helps—and it is truly the opposite of what my mind is telling me. You can only do so much; but the biggest word of advice I can give is not to give up on someone who is desperately trying not to give up on himself. Encourage the person to be consistent in getting professional help so that you can stay in friend status, not counselor status. For example, on many days, a strong hug is so healing. I go through life feeling like I've got a bad sunburn emotionally; and the depression and anorexia want to steal all God has for me—like someone poking my sunburn all day. Hugs and words of encouragement about the hope and future God has for me are hopeful and soothing. It takes love and character to handle struggles with courage, integrity, and obedience. Recovery isn't perfect! God chooses to look into and love our hearts, especially when we seek Him. Even in the midst of your own fight, seek to encourage another. This is one reason why I write. It's just *not* only about me! Most days I try to trust that, as I reach out to others, He's taking care of me and mine. Ask God for His guidance, and reach out. Finally, and personally, when a friend says nothing to me, I feel invisible—and I don't need help with that. I'm trying with all the strength God gives me to be present. Remember my verse? It's a great and bold one to share because it evokes a commitment: "I will not die, but live, and will proclaim what the Lord has done" (Ps. 118:17). Let's ask God to give us words of hope and the courage to be in one another's lives.

Thank you for letting me share my heart. Thank you for hanging with me while I explain the reason behind my sharing. I never want to belittle you, whatever path God has us on. God wants us to lift each other up as we learn more about one another. We are not ignorant people! We just need some direction to reach out, especially when we have no idea where to start. I sure do! God has had this on my heart…and this is what I wanted you to know.

Love to you,
Stacee

References

The Cutting Truth
Warner, Anna B. Jesus Loves Me. Public Domain, 1860.

You Are Worth Saving
Lowry, Robert. Nothing But The Blood. Public Domain, 1876.

Geese, the Pond and God
Sarah Young, Jesus Calling (Nashville, TN: Thomas Nelson, 2004), 261.

The Skinny on Shame
Mote, Edward. My Hope is Built on Nothing Less. Public Domain, 1834.

Grab The Trunk
Author Unknown. "The Oak Tree."

The Truth Is
"Get the Facts on Eating Disorders," The National Eating Disorder Association, https://www.nationaleatingdisorders.org/get-facts-eating-disorders.

Daigle, Lauren. "Trust in You." How Can It Be. Franklin, Washington: Centricity Music, 2015.

Valley Girl
Young, Jesus Calling, 235.

Relentless
Young, Jesus Calling, 175.

What I Want You to Know
"Nine Truths About Eating Disorders," The National Eating Disorder Association, https://www.nationaleatingdisorders.org/blog/nine-truths-about-eating-disorders.

**For More information on Eating Disorders, please visit the National Eating Disorders Association website: www.nationaleating-disorders.org.

About the Author

Stacee Goetzinger is a writer, speaker, wife, mother, daughter, and friend. I will not die but live, and proclaim what the Lord has done (Psalm 118:17) is her life verse and describes her passion to allow God to use the pain of a lengthy battle with mental illness and an eating disorder to write and speak words of hope, courage, and life. Stacee came to faith in Jesus at a young age, but experiencing God's unconditional love was a constant struggle, always feeling instead the need to somehow prove she was acceptable and worthy of being loved. As an adult, an eating disorder, held in check for a number of years, no longer was manageable, and Stacee quickly found herself in the depths of depression, anorexia, and other means of self-harm. In the midst of that pain and darkness, God spoke into her heart and mind a life-changing picture of hope and life. One which, for the first time, helped Stacee undeniably see and feel God's unconditional love and acceptance. God continues to restore Stacee's life and has given her a message of hope she is eager to share. For those struggling with issues like hers or just struggling through the journey of life, Stacee's hope is that out of her experience of pain and triumph, she is able to encourage and point others to the life-giving love, forgiveness, and hope which only come from God, the Father's, heart. Stacee loves being the wife to her supportive husband Doug and mom to her redheaded encouragers, Shelbee and Rylee. Stacee and her family live in Oklahoma City, Oklahoma. You can connect with Stacee and catch her latest blog post at www.speakoutloud.me.

CPSIA information can be obtained
at www.ICGtesting.com
Printed in the USA
FSHW010701080521
81131FS